NEW DIRECTIONS FOR TEACHING AND LEARNING

Robert J. Menges, *Northwestern University*
EDITOR-IN-CHIEF

Marilla D. Svinicki, *University of Texas, Austin*
ASSOCIATE EDITOR

Interdisciplinary Studies Today

Julie Thompson Klein
Wayne State University

William G. Doty
University of Alabama, Tuscaloosa

EDITORS

Number 58, Summer 1994

JOSSEY-BASS PUBLISHERS
San Francisco

INTERDISCIPLINARY STUDIES TODAY
Julie Thompson Klein, William G. Doty (eds.)
New Directions for Teaching and Learning, no. 58
Robert J. Menges, Editor-in-Chief
Marilla D. Svinicki, Associate Editor

Microfilm copies of issues and articles are available in 16mm and 35mm, as well as microfiche in 105mm, through University Microfilms Inc., 300 North Zeeb Road, Ann Arbor, Michigan 48106-1346.

LC 85-644763   ISSN 0271-0633   ISBN 0-7879-9974-1

NEW DIRECTIONS FOR TEACHING AND LEARNING is part of The Jossey-Bass Higher and Adult Education Series and is published quarterly by Jossey-Bass Inc., Publishers, 350 Sansome Street, San Francisco, California 94104-1342. Second-class postage paid at San Francisco, California, and at additional mailing offices. POSTMASTER: Send address changes to New Directions for Teaching and Learning, Jossey-Bass Inc., Publishers, 350 Sansome Street, San Francisco, California 94104-1342.

SUBSCRIPTIONS for 1994 cost $47.00 for individuals and $62.00 for institutions, agencies, and libraries.

EDITORIAL CORRESPONDENCE should be sent to the editor-in-chief, Robert J. Menges, Northwestern University, Center for the Teaching Professions, 2003 Sheridan Road, Evanston, Illinois 60208-2610.

Cover photograph by Richard Blair/Color & Light © 1990.

Manufactured in the United States of America. Nearly all Jossey-Bass books, jackets, and periodicals are printed on recycled paper that contains at least 50 percent recycled waste, including 10 percent postconsumer waste. Many of our materials are also printed with vegetable-based inks; during the printing process, these inks emit fewer volatile organic compounds (VOCs) than petroleum-based inks. VOCs contribute to the formation of smog.

CONTENTS

About This Publication. Since 1980, *New Directions for Teaching and Learning (NDTL)* has brought a unique blend of theory, research, and practice to leaders in postsecondary education. *NDTL* sourcebooks strive not only for solid substance but also for timeliness, compactness, and accessibility.

The series has four goals: to inform readers about current and future directions in teaching and learning in postsecondary education; to illuminate the context that shapes these new directions; to illustrate these new directions through examples from real settings; and to propose ways in which these new directions can be incorporated into still other settings.

This publication reflects our view that teaching deserves respect as a high form of scholarship. We believe that significant scholarship is conducted not only by researchers who report results of empirical investigations but also by practitioners who share disciplined reflections about teaching. Contributors to *NDTL* approach questions of teaching and learning as seriously as they approach substantive questions in their own disciplines, and they deal not only with pedagogical issues but also with the intellectual and social context in which these issues arise. Authors deal on the one hand with theory and research and on the other with practice, and they translate from research and theory to practice and back again.

About This Volume. For the present volume, Julie Thompson Klein and William G. Doty have assembled chapters that map the terrain of interdisciplinary studies today. Chapter One surveys the intellectual roots of interdisciplinary studies. The remaining chapters blend theory and research with practice as they examine the design, administration, and assessment of interdisciplinary courses and programs. Chapter Five relates networking to the interdisciplinary enterprise. Klein and Doty thank the authors for offering a rich resource to those who work in interdisciplinary education today.

Robert J. Menges, *Editor-in-Chief*
Marilla D. Svinicki, *Associate Editor*

ROBERT J. MENGES, *editor-in-chief, is professor of education and social policy at Northwestern University, and senior researcher, National Center on Post-secondary Teaching, Learning, and Assessment.*

MARILLA D. SVINICKI, *associate editor, is director of the Center for Teaching Effectiveness, University of Texas at Austin.*

EDITORS' NOTES

The word *interdisciplinary* attracts many minds and hearts. For the disciplinarian working on a complex problem or question, it may represent a new method or concept. For the college administrator, it can be a strategy for grouping subdisciplines into a program or for responding quickly to new interests and demands. It can demarcate new cross-departmental programs, hybrid fields of knowledge, and new interdisciplines. And it is a handy label for new fields of study. Issues in medical ethics and genetic engineering, post–Civil War police systems that have implications for contemporary treatment of drug-related illnesses, and mathematical models of musical composition that hold out the promise of computer-generated music are just a few of the many areas in the practice and production of knowledge that exemplify contemporary interdisciplinary studies (IDS).

Outside academe, interdisciplinarity has a long history that spans problem-solving teams in pharmaceutical, aeronautical, agricultural, engineering, and technology systems, and it is increasingly being applied in commercial and communications contexts. Here, interdisciplinary praxis is often not something extra, not a matter to be defended and structured, but the essence of the enterprise as a whole. In such interdisciplinary situations, the favored collaborator is not the most highly trained specialist but the person who can work most cooperatively with others. The skills most sought after include: sharing perspectives from individual bailiwicks, reflecting a common problem through the perspectives supplied by other disciplines, rethinking one's own individual skills and perspectives in terms of a shared objective, and going beyond merely compiling additive information (say, by adding medical to demographic data) to devise a truly integrative solution whose contours do not match those derived from any single disciplinary source. The best interdisciplinarian avoids the free-for-all struggle to dominate the enterprise and apply its gains to a particular disciplinary perspective or proprietary research project so that the end results are applicable to multiple fields.

Interdisciplinary approaches—whether in the archive or field site, the classroom or laboratory, the invisible college, or the established discipline—involve reciprocity across specializations as well as willingness to think through one's position in order to contribute to the larger interest of a reformulated common goal. Unfortunately, the contemporary context emphasizes distinctive individualism and classroom competition; the IDS approaches are now consequently unfamiliar. Over the long term, higher education has promoted increased specialization and fragmentation, which impede and sometimes directly undermine methodological collaboration and cross-fertilization among various approaches to the interpretation of data or problem solving. A number of campaigns have sought both to combat problems created by overspecialization and to foster interdisciplinary objectives in the academic curriculum. These campaigns have ranged from the general education reforms of the first half of the twentieth century to the radical educational experiments of the 1960s and 1970s (such as the free university movements) and the current plurality of interdisciplinary traditions and innovations. These efforts have produced approaches ranging from disciplinary foci supplemented by background information from several disciplines, to multidisciplinary juxtapositions of different perspectives on a common topic, to genuinely interdisciplinary integration of different approaches (usually worked out collaboratively from the inception of the IDS project, not just taped together from various unrelated findings), and finally to what may be called *transdisciplinary* concepts and paradigms that are increasingly understood as applicable globally across several spheres of knowledge and technology.

To be sure, something as advanced as transdisciplinary methods may be unfamiliar in many venues, but the field of interdisciplinary studies is currently experiencing a resurgence of interest across multiple sectors, ranging from K–12 schooling to undergraduate general education, honors programs, and area studies programs; to interdisciplinary fields, specialties, and schools; and to graduate research projects and postgraduate professional and applied technology programs. Of course, such interest builds on earlier academic experiments and educational experiences, but it also responds to new demands for integrated approaches to complex social and technological problems as well as to changes in the forms and structures of contemporary intellectual activity. The widespread assertion that knowledge has become increasingly interdisciplinary underscores these changes. Such an assertion is repeated across the disciplines of the humanities, social sciences, natural sciences, and technology as well as in national reports on the state of the university and in prognoses of what competence in education will mean for the twenty-first century.

The current multiplicity of types of interdisciplinary activities, their increasing visibility and legitimacy, and the growing scholarly literature are strong testimonies to the health of IDS. Nonetheless, many teachers and administrators are uncertain about the best way to proceed on their own campuses. This sourcebook addresses their needs. We seek to enable interdisciplinarity by helping readers to use approaches to learning that identify the developmental continuum ranging from disciplinary segmentation to multidisciplinary alignment and transdisciplinary integration and application of results. We hope to facilitate administrative support of the latter, to strengthen arguments for interdisciplinary approaches, and to provide resources for the ongoing evaluation and assessment of IDS projects and programs.

The authors of the chapters in this volume are all highly experienced in interdisciplinary contexts—as scholars, teachers, administrators, and consultants—and their focus here is less on highly abstract intellectual language borrowed from contemporary critical theorists (such as that of Michel Foucault, Roland Barthes, or Jacques Derrida) than it is on ways of making interdisciplinary studies a reality on particular campuses in specific academic locales, large or small. The authors focus on interdisciplinary practice as the facilitation and enablement of what might otherwise remain only frustratingly theoretical. Hence, the book synthesizes theoretical understanding, research findings, and practical strategies with an emphasis on undergraduate education in the United States. By using concrete instances to illustrate the various types of programs and courses, the book provides models both for the strengthening of curricular structures and for pedagogical approaches in several types of academic settings.

The Origins of This Volume

Although this *New Directions* sourcebook makes its own unique contributions, the original catalyst for this volume deserves mention. Over a three-year period beginning in 1989, the Association of American Colleges (AAC) (1991–92) sponsored a major study called "Liberal Learning and the Arts and Sciences Major." The study was funded by the Ford Foundation and the Department of Education's Fund for the Improvement of Postsecondary Education (FIPSE). Twelve learned societies were invited to head national task forces charged with investigating the nature, sequencing, and effectiveness of undergraduate majors in biology, economics, history, interdisciplinary studies, mathematics, philosophy, physics, political science, psychology, religious studies, sociology, and women's studies. Because of its long-standing interest in interdisciplinary issues, the Society for Values in Higher Education (SVHE) was invited to head the task force on interdisciplinary studies. In keeping with their charge, the members of the SVHE task force studied program models, surveyed appropriate professional groups, hosted information-gathering panels at national meetings, and compiled a final report (Association of American Colleges, 1992–93). William G. Doty of the University of Alabama/Tuscaloosa served as chair and scribe. The task force included SVHE members Alice F. Carse of Old Westbury, Edward Ordman of Memphis State University, and Constance D. Ramirez of Duquesne University. They were joined by Julie Thompson Klein of Wayne State University and the Association for Integrative Studies (AIS), a national professional organization for interdisciplinarians.

Recognizing that there was no authoritative national report on IDS, the SVHE task force heeded the AAC's admonition to distribute the full text of its report to constituent professional groups. The SVHE and the AIS joined forces in this effort, and the result was *Interdisciplinary Resources*, a special issue of the AIS journal *Issues in Integrative Studies* (Doty and Klein, 1990). Distributed to all AIS members and to interested SVHE fellows and others, the issue contained the complete text of the SVHE task force report, as well as contributions from leading national experts in the areas of scholarly resources, curriculum development, program administration, and organizational networking. In keeping with the mandate of *New Directions in Teaching and Learning*, the current sourcebook updates and refocuses the earlier effort in ways that emphasize the practice—the doing—of IDS. In response to demand from practitioners, the editors invited three experts in interdisciplinary assessment to contribute to the current effort.

The authors of the chapters in this volume have taken several recommendations of the SVHE task force report to heart. [For a copy of the report, see Doty and Klein, 1990 (now out of print); Association of American Colleges, 1991, pp. 61–76 (a collection of condensed versions of all of the task force results).] For example, the task force advised IDS program directors and faculty to emphasize formal preparation of instructors and continuing reevaluation of common interdisciplinary enterprises. It also encouraged them to organize programs and courses in ways that reflected the necessary triangulation of depth, breadth, and synthesis—a process that can ensure that the knowledge produced is truly integrative and that student performance is developed consistently across the IDS curriculum. The contributions to this volume take both recommendations into account.

The current volume responds to task force recommendations in two other ways: The task force urged administrators and curriculum committees to work toward integrating interdisciplinary activities in campuswide planning, programming, and funding at all administrative levels. That emphasis is evident here. The task force also urged campus leaders to articulate and develop relationships with other campus programs and to take care that faculty members not be penalized for their involvement in IDS when tenure, promotion, and salary decisions are made. Other recommendations reflected in this volume include the establishment of support networks across programs (and, on a large campus, among dispersed offerings) and the establishment of liaisons with library and bibliographic personnel in order to provide the broadest possible base of research in publications and data compilations. Networking across national interdisciplinary organizations, including those focused on general education or first-year curricula, honors programs, and various Studies programs (such as American, Women or Gender, Medieval and Renaissance, and so on) is another crucial practical element, and it, too, is emphasized here.

The Resources in This Volume

The current volume goes beyond core definitions, surveys of program types, and the history of interdisciplinary studies, which, as Julie Thompson Klein notes in Chapter One, have all been treated in a number of published sources. She defines entry points into pertinent scholarly literatures and advises on the use of electronic information systems and individual networking strategies that can be helpful in locating less visible and emergent resources.

In Chapter Two, William Newell focuses on issues encountered in the process of designing interdisciplinary courses. These issues range from determining the format and designing syllabi to organizing teaching teams and devising appropriate pedagogies. In Chapter Three, Beth Casey formulates a set of administrative principles sensitive to the unique demands of differing program structures and institutional politics. In Chapter Four, Michael Field, Russell Lee, and Mary Lee Field join forces to provide the first published synthesis of research findings, lessons from exemplary models, and recommendations based on actual practice of interdisciplinary assessment. And in Chapter Five, Nelson Bingham advises on the ways in which the members of interdisciplinary organizations can nurture and support one another.

The riches in these chapters reflect the fact that interdisciplinary courses, programs, centers, and schools have had an enormous impact on recent campus intellectual life. Interdisciplinary projects promote interaction between student and faculty learners, bridge administrative units, and foster synthesis of different forms of knowledge while serendipitously encouraging lively discussion across all parts of a campus, an effect especially evident when IDS centers provide public lectures and seminars as well as opportunities for advanced faculty research. Students often discover in these centers that much of their future work activities will involve working cooperatively in similar situations, and college faculty often discover that their own production of knowledge can be immeasurably advanced by contacts with other sympathetic workers whom they otherwise might not encounter.

As far as advocacy for such interdisciplinary atmospheres is concerned, this volume in effect puts wheels on the collected body of wisdom and experience regarding IDS. It shares the wealth of ideas, strategies, and practical approaches that practitioners across the nation are using at all parts of the interdisciplinary life cycle within a rich variety of institutional settings and curricular contexts.

For the editors, this volume is the culminating step in a collaboration over several years. We thank the Association of American Colleges, the Ford Foundation, and the FIPSE for making the work of the original SVHE task force possible, and they acknowledge the institutional support received from the SVHE and the AIS in data gathering and analysis and the eventual published results of the task force. The editors are grateful to the many institutions whose staff shared examples of good and bad practice and information about their experiences with IDS. Finally, they thank the series editors, Robert Menges and Marilla Svinicki, for their advice in helping them to share the cumulative fruits of these labors and the collective wisdom of the authors with a wide national audience.

Julie Thompson Klein
William G. Doty
Editors

References

Association of American Colleges. *Liberal Learning and the Arts and Sciences Major.* Washington, D.C.: Association of American Colleges, 1991.

Doty, W. G., and Klein, J. T. (eds.). "Interdisciplinary Resources" (special issue). *Issues in Integrative Studies*, 1990, 8.

JULIE THOMPSON KLEIN *is professor of humanities in the Interdisciplinary Studies Program at Wayne State University. A former editor of the journal* Issues in Integrative Studies *and former president of the Association for Integrative Studies, she has published widely on interdisciplinary research and studies.*

WILLIAM G. DOTY *is professor of humanities in the Department of Religious Studies at the University of Alabama Tuscaloosa, where he has taught in the interdisciplinary New College. Former national coordinator of the American Academy of Religion's annual competition for the best publication in the field, he has published extensively on myth and ritual, men's studies, classics, and religious studies. He is a regular writer for* Art Papers (Atlanta).

By combining new and traditional approaches to the locating of interdisciplinary knowledge and information, educators can utilize the full range of existing resources while periodically updating their personal and institutional collections.

Finding Interdisciplinary Knowledge and Information

Julie Thompson Klein

Interdisciplinary studies (IDS) generate needs for knowledge and information that span program administration, curriculum development, pedagogy, assessment, and a staggering variety of interdisciplinary activities. Filling these needs is no small order. Resources are dispersed across books and articles, conference presentations, institutional working papers and internal reports, course syllabi, software, and audio and visual media as well as the vast body of oral wisdom on the subject. Locating these resources requires the use of both published literatures and information-seeking strategies. The literatures span major works on IDS as well as disciplinary and interdisciplinary fields of knowledge. The strategies include on-line data base searching as well as electronic and personal networking. By combining these approaches, teachers and administrators can build and periodically update their personal and institutional collections.

Starting Out in IDS

The first two kinds of resources that teachers and administrators want are an introductory overview and curricular models and sample syllabi. There are several broad-based introductions beyond the current sourcebook.

For their assistance in devising strategies and identifying resources, I thank Joan Fiscella, bibliographer for professional studies at the library of the University of Illinois at Chicago, and Stacey Kimmel, special projects librarian at Miami University libraries.

To begin with, Mayville surveys fundamental definitions, educational models, and program types:

- Mayville, William. *Interdisciplinarity: The Mutable Paradigm.* AAHE-ERIC Higher Education Research Report No. 9. Washington, D.C.: American Association for Higher Education, 1978.

Three book chapters also survey the topic:

- Halliburton, David. "Interdisciplinary Studies." In Arthur Chickering (ed.), *The Modern American College.* San Francisco: Jossey-Bass, 1981.
- Klein, Julie Thompson."I.D.S." *Interdisciplinarity: History, Theory, and Practice.* Detroit: Wayne State University Press, 1990.
- Klein, Julie Thompson, and William Newell. "Interdisciplinary Studies."In Jerry Gaff and James Ratcliff (eds.), *Handbook on the Undergraduate Curriculum.* San Francisco: Jossey-Bass, forthcoming.

Halliburton reviews core definitions, curricular types, organizational issues, the value of interdisciplinary approaches, and their significance for adult learners. Klein examines major issues and characteristics in models ranging from universities, colleges, and graduate programs to core curricula, clustered and single courses, and independent studies. Klein and Newell survey the current state of the art in a comprehensive overview of purposes, theory, trends, strategies, practices, criteria, outcomes, and barriers. In addition, Newell's directory of undergraduate interdisciplinary programs, the most current compilation of interdisciplinary programs in the United States, is an excellent place to start the search for peer programs, sample syllabi, and consultants:

- Newell, William H. *Interdisciplinary Undergraduate Programs: A Directory.* Oxford, Ohio: Association for Integrative Studies, 1986.

Strategies and arguments comprise a vital dimension of interdisciplinary knowledge. Two articles provide insight into how individuals behave in interdisciplinary contexts:

- Kann, Mark. "The Political Culture of Interdisciplinary Explanation." *Humanities in Society,* 1979, 2(3), 185–200.
- Gaff, Jerry, and Robert Wilson. "Faculty Cultures and Interdisciplinary Studies." *Journal of Higher Education,* 1971, 42(3), 186–201.

Beyond Chapter Three by Beth Casey in this volume of *New Directions for Teaching and Learning,* two additional items aid in formulating program strategies:

- Benson, Thomas. "Five Arguments Against Interdisciplinary Studies." *Issues in Integrative Studies,* 1982, 1, 38–48.
- Klein, Julie Thompson. "Interdisciplinary Futures." In *Crossing Boundaries: Knowledge, Disciplinarities, and Interdisciplinarities.* Charlottesville: University Press of Virginia, forthcoming.

Klein examines current strategies for enabling interdisciplinary research and education on campus. An additional work by Gaff, although not focused directly on IDS, remains a useful compilation of advice readily adaptable to interdisciplinary general education programs:

- Gaff, Jerry. "Avoiding the Potholes: Strategies for Reforming General Education." *Educational Record*, 1980, *61*(4), 50–59.

Understanding interdisciplinary process is equally important. Going beyond Chapters Two and Four in this volume, Newell draws on the experience of Miami University's School of Interdisciplinary Studies to explain the process of interdisciplinary teaching and learning:

- Newell, William. "Academic Disciplines and Undergraduate Interdisciplinary Education." *European Journal of Education*, 1992, 27(3), 211–221.

Although the work of Hursh, Haas, and Moore is rooted in a specific context, it is an adaptable model for interdisciplinary study of a given problem:

- Hursh, Barbara, Paul Haas, and Michael Moore. "An Interdisciplinary Model to Implement General Education." *Journal of Higher Education*, 1983, *54*, 42–59.

Two other models illuminate interdisciplinary process:

- DeWachter, Maurice. "Interdisciplinary Bioethics? But Where Do We Start? A Reflection on Epochè as Method." *Journal of Medicine and Philosophy*, 1982, 7(3), 275–287.
- Klein, Julie Thompson. "Applying Interdisciplinary Models to Design, Planning, and Policy Making." *Knowledge and Policy*, 1990–1991, 3(4), 29–55.

Hursh, Haas, and Moore build on the work of Dewey, Piaget, and Perry. DeWachter draws on bioethics, while Klein presents a global model for interdisciplinary research and problem solving.

Although reflections on the philosophy of IDS run throughout the core literature on interdisciplinarity, four items deserve special mention:

- Taylor, Alastair. "Integrative Principles and the Educational Process." *Main Currents in Modern Thought*, 1969, 25(5), 126–133.
- Pring, Richard. "Curriculum Integration." *Proceedings of the Philosophy of Education Society of Great Britain*, 1971, 5(2), 170–200.
- Doyal, Len. "Interdisciplinary Studies in Higher Education." *Universities Quarterly, Higher Education and Society*, 1974, 28(4), 470–487.
- Phenix, Philip. "Use of the Disciplines as Curriculum Content." *Educational Forum*, 1962, *26*, 273–280.

Drawing on the pioneering work of the Foundation for Integrative Education, Taylor contrasts *integration* as a synthesis of presently accepted postulates with the *integrative* building of new conceptual models. Building on a distinction between interdisciplinary and integrated conceptions of the curriculum, Pring appraises proposals for integrating the curriculum, including a *strong thesis*, an implicit belief in the unity of knowledge, and a *weak thesis*, a more limited claim for unity in broad fields of experience. Doyal assesses three different theories of IDS (the pragmatic approach, the methods and concepts approach, and the large integrative scheme), while Phenix considers the use of disciplines as curriculum content.

Three additional items belong on any introductory reading list:

- Armstrong, Forrest. "Faculty Development through Interdisciplinarity." *JGE: The Journal of General Education*, 1980, *32*(1), 52–63.
- Trow, Martin. "Interdisciplinary Studies as a Counterculture: Problems of Birth, Growth, and Survival." *Issues in Integrative Studies*, 1984–1985, *4*, 1–15.
- White, Alvin (ed.). *Interdisciplinary Teaching*. New Directions for Teaching and Learning no. 8. San Francisco: Jossey-Bass, 1981.

Armstrong defines four major levels of integration in IDS and its role in faculty and institutional development. Trow analyzes interdisciplinary programs founded in the 1960s and 1970s and draws important lessons about program life cycle. Finally, the earlier *New Directions for Teaching and Learning* sourcebook on IDS, edited by White, is less an overview of the subject than a collection of individual accounts and reflections.

Finding Models and Syllabi

Finding models and syllabi requires familiarity with core literatures and online data base searching as well as electronic and personal networking. Throughout this process, four principles apply. First, a defunct model is not necessarily an invalid model. Second, a model or syllabus is rarely adopted wholesale. Instead, it is adapted to local strengths and limitations. Third, establishing a good working relationship with local library personnel is crucial. Fourth, following the less obvious path of peripheral networking will yield excellent results.

Courses and programs falter for a number of reasons, not the least of which are departure of key personnel, financial strain, and shifts in political climates. Knowing why courses and programs have encountered difficulties on particular campuses is important but should not deter from using imported models and syllabi if, to invoke the second principle, faculty and administrators respect their own institutional cultures. Fortunately, a cornucopia of models exists.

The genre that dominates the IDS literature is the case study, a form that incorporates individual stories, program and course descriptions, and strategies and reflections. There are literally thousands of case studies dispersed across disciplinary, professional, and interdisciplinary literatures. Their variety is astonishing, as a brief list indicates: teaching bioethics, using economics in problem-oriented programs, combining learning and teaching styles in an engineering-rhetoric course, teaching technology to nontechnology students, comparing the nature of physics and history, basing a course in a national park, providing environmental education for nonscience majors, teaching the philosophy and physics of space and time, linking geology with prehistoric archaeology, teaching chemical evolution to undergraduates, exploring relations between physics and biology, and devising integrative approaches to values education, nuclear education, and community studies. Case studies are accessible in four sometimes overlapping forms: collected conference papers, collected program reports, special issues of journals, and publications from organizations with interdisciplinary interests.

Published Collections. Program models, course descriptions and syllabi, reading lists, and practical advice often appear in collections of conference papers. For example, George Mason University sponsors a national conference on nontraditional and interdisciplinary programs. Conference papers appear on microfiche in the ERIC system. ERIC is the acronym for Educational Resources Information Center, a nationwide family of information clearinghouses sponsored by the U.S. Department of Education. Many college and university libraries maintain an ERIC fiche collection, and photocopies of many documents can be ordered directly from ERIC. Papers from the 1987 and 1989 George Mason University meetings were not published, and there was no meeting in 1993. Sets of fiche for other years are obtainable as follows: ED 287 427, ED 287 435, ED 287 426 (1983); ED 287 425 (1984); ED 287 434 (1985); ED 287 424 (1986); ED 297 647 (1988); ED 333 852 (1990); ED 333 853 (1991); ED 346 789 (1992).

Collections of papers from single meetings and anthologies of essays also contain models. Milicic presents a variety of perspectives on a single campus:
- Milicic, Vladimir (ed.). *Symposium on Interdisciplinary Aspects of Academic Disciplines*. Bellingham: Western Washington University, 1973.

Two additional collections place a strong emphasis on the humanities:
- Dill, Stephen (ed.). *Integrated Studies: Challenges to the College Curriculum*. Washington, D.C.: University Press of America, 1982.
- Clark, Mark E., and Roger Johnson, Jr. (eds.). *Curricular Reform: Narratives of Interdisciplinary Humanities Programs*. Chattanooga, Tenn.: Southern Humanities Press, 1991.

Clark and Wawrytko have also collected papers from a national conference:
- Clark, Mary E., and Sandra A. Wawrytko (eds.). *Rethinking the Curriculum: Toward an Integrated, Interdisciplinary College Education*. New York: Greenwood Press, 1990.

Because there is no single location where IDS bibliography is systematically and regularly updated, monitoring journals and newsletters enables new references to be caught as they emerge. The major sites include the newsletter of the Association for Integrative Studies (AIS), *Issues in Integrative Studies* (the AIS journal), *Improving College and University Teaching, Change, Liberal Education* (the journal of the Association of American Colleges and Universities), *Perspectives* (the journal of the Association of General and Liberal Studies), *Interdisciplinary Humanities* (the journal of the National Association for Humanities Education), and the *Journal of Interdisciplinary Studies* (published by the International Christian Studies Association). A number of special journal issues and sections within issues have also been devoted to interdisciplinary topics over the past two decades:

- "Curriculum: Interdisciplinary Insights." *Teacher's College Record*, 1971, 73(2).
- "Interdisciplinary Education." *Liberal Education*, Spring 1979.
- "Experimental Interdisciplinary Programs." *Soundings: An Interdisciplinary Journal*, 1981, 54(1).
- "Creating an Integrated Curriculum: The 'Higher' in Higher Education." *Current Issues in Higher Education*, 1981, 2. (ED 213 324)
  (Note especially Mary Jim Josephs, "Curricular Integration: Mortar for the Ivory Tower," pp. 5–8, with comments on the link between IDS and skills development.)
- "Interdisciplinary Studies." *Improving College and University Teaching*, 1982, 30(1).
- "Crossing the Boundaries." *Forum for Liberal Education*, 1986, 8(4). (ED 266 758)
- "Interdisciplinary Studies: Defining and Defending." *National Forum*, 1989, 69(2).
- "Interdisciplinary Studies." *Change Magazine*, August 1978. (ED 157 461)
- "Interdisciplinary Studies." *European Journal of Education*, 1992, 27(3).

European collections have a dual function for the U.S. audience: they are excellent sources of case studies and analyses, and they provide entry into the European literatures. The major collections span two decades. The Organization for Economic Cooperation and Development (OECD) sponsored international symposia in 1970 and 1984:

- Organization for Economic Cooperation and Development. *Interdisciplinarity: Problems of Teaching and Research in Universities*. Paris: OECD, 1972.
- Organization for Economic Cooperation and Development. *Interdisciplinarity Revisited: Reassessing the Concept in the Light of Institutional Experience*. Stockholm: OECD, Swedish National Board of Universities and Colleges, and Linköping University, 1985.

The results of work conducted under the auspices of the Group for Research and Innovation in Higher Education (GRIHE), which was affiliated with the Nuffield Foundation, have been published since 1975:

- Case Studies in Interdisciplinarity. London: GRIHE, Nuffield Foundation. (Printed by the University of York.)
- Vol. 1: Environmental Sciences and Engineering, Sept. 1975.
- Vol. 2: Science, Technology and Society, Oct. 1975.
- Vol. 3: Integrated Social Sciences, Sept. 1975
- Vol. 4: National and International Studies, Sept. 1975
- Vol. 5: Humanities and Cognitive Studies, Sept. 1975.

The proceedings of a symposium on interdisciplinary courses in Europe held at City University in London are available in the United States from ERIC under the title *Interdisciplinarity* (ED 165 512). In addition, GRIHE published:

- *Interdisciplinarity: A Report by the Group for Research and Innovation*. Regents Park, England: Nuffield Foundation, July 1975.

The results of a conference on interdisciplinarity in higher education held under UNESCO auspices in Bucharest in 1983 are also available from ERIC:
- Hanisch, Thor, and Wolfgang Vollman (eds.). *Interdisciplinarity in Higher Education.* Bucharest, Romania: European Center for Higher Education, 1983. (ED 249 864)

The European literature is accessible in several other places as well. Two special journal issues illuminate the current climate for interdisciplinary work in Europe, especially in Britain, Germany, and Switzerland:
- "Interdisciplinary Studies," *European Journal of Education,* 1992, 27(3) (entire issue).
- "Disciplinary Cultures," *European Journal of Education,* 1990, 35(3) (entire issue).

Another special issue of *Issues in Integrative Studies* features current interdisciplinary research and education along with a reprint of S. N. Smirnov's "The Main Forms of Interdisciplinary Development of Modern Science":
- "Interdisciplinarity: European Perspectives." *Issues in Integrative Studies,* 1994, 12 (entire issue).

Accounts of research at the University of Bielefeld's Center for Interdisciplinary Research are available to the U.S. audience from two sources:
- Vosskamp, Wilhelm. "From Scientific Specialization to the Dialogue between the Disciplines." *Issues in Integrative Studies,* 1986, 4, 17–36.
- Sjölander, Sverre. "Long-Term and Short-Term Interdisciplinary Work." In Organization for Economic Cooperation and Development, *Interdisciplinarity Revisited: Reassessing the Concept in the Light of Institutional Experience.* Stockholm: OECD, Swedish National Board of Universities and Colleges, and Linköping University, 1985.

Networking. In the past, many educators went no farther than their local libraries. Networking widens the yield. Networking is a multilayered activity that encompasses familiar person-to-person forms of social contact through correspondence, telephone calls, and personal meetings as well as the rich resources of electronic communication, which range from interinstitutional conversations and viewing library holdings to downloading texts and gathering references on the rapidly expanding information highway. Combining networking with electronic searching is the best means of ensuring steady access to existing and emerging resources. Some material is available in most college and university libraries, but a significant portion may have to be obtained through interlibrary loan and networking. Here is where the third and fourth principles—establishing a good working relationship with local library personnel and realizing that peripheral yields may be as valuable as traditional bibliography—apply. Developing personal contacts is also essential, a strategy that includes both broad-based organizations and specialized groups.

The Association for Integrative Studies (AIS) is a national professional organization for interdisciplinarians. Its annual meetings facilitate individual and interest group networking. The organization's membership directory is an excellent source of individual contacts and peer programs. The AIS quarterly newsletter publishes descriptions of programs and courses as well as noting the appearance of pertinent reports and studies. Miami University's School of Interdisciplinary Studies is the administrative home of both the AIS and the Institute in Integrative Studies, a organization funded by FIPSE to offer seminars and workshops providing in-depth experience in interdisciplinary methodology, pedagogy, and curriculum design. The AIS also sponsors INTERDIS Computer List, an open, electronic E-mail conversation. Requests for program models, sample syllabi, answers to questions, and bibliography are welcome, as is information about new bibliography, other resources, and networking contacts. To participate, send an E-mail message to Listserv@miamiu.acs.muohio.edu. The body of the message should read SUB INTERDIS<your name>. Phone numbers and personnel change through the years, but having a reliable place to begin is crucial in obtaining any kind of information. For more details on the electronic conversation, send an E-mail message to Wolfe_Chris@msmail.muohio.edu. If Wolfe is not available contact William Newell at the E-mail address or telephone number given in the next paragraph.

Miami University maintains two additional sets of resources, one located at the AIS office and the other in the university's library system. The AIS archives house a multitude of syllabi generated by the Institute and collected by Newell when compiling the directory of undergraduate interdisciplinary programs mentioned earlier. The archives also contain such buried treasures as the report of a FIPSE-funded project on altering existing general education courses with interdisciplinary learning objectives in mind:

• *Creating Connections: An Experiment in Interdisciplinary Education*. Wichita, Kans.: Wichita State University, 1981–1984.

For questions about access to the archives and information on the AIS and the Institute, contact the AIS executive director, William Newell, at the School of Interdisciplinary Studies, Miami University, Oxford, Ohio 45056 (telephone: 513–529–2213; fax: 513–529–5849). Newell's Internet address is newell_Bill@msmail.muohio.edu, or leave a telephone voice mail message.

Finally, the Miami University libraries system has built up a collection of materials that can serve as a defining touchstone for collection building in other institutions. The on-line catalogue is called SHERLOCK. To access SHERLOCK via Internet, telnet to Miamilink.Lib.muohio.edu. Interdisciplinary material appears under many subject headings, but the most fruitful for searching purposes are *interdisciplinary approach in education* and *interdisciplinary approach to knowledge*. In case of technical difficulties, contact the reference desk at 513–529–4141, and ask for the current liaison to the School of Interdisciplinary Studies .

Three additional organizations serve interdisciplinary educators. Since 1953, the Association for Core Curriculum has been serving all levels, although its special focus is middle schools. The tradition of interdisciplinary units in middle and high schools dates from the core curriculum movement of the

1930s and 1940s. For further information about the organization and its quarterly newsletter, *The Core Teacher*, contact Gordon Vars, its executive secretary and treasurer, at the Department of Teaching, Leadership, and Curriculum Studies, 404 White Hall, Kent State University, Kent OH 44242–0001 (tel.: 216–672–2580). Note, relatedly, that Marcella Kysilka is currently completing a new book on interdisciplinary curriculum at the K-12 levels. Forthcoming from Eye on Education, the book covers definitions of and historical perspectives on integrated curricula, with models for curriculum planning. The National Association of Humanities Education (NAHE) serves middle school through adult graduate liberal studies, with an added special interest in museum education. The NAHE holds biennial meetings at which informal consultations can be arranged, and its journal, *Interdisciplinary Humanities* (formerly called *Humanities Education*), is now indexed in ERIC. For information, contact its executive secretary, Dr. Fred Schroeder, at the Department of Interdisciplinary Programs, University of Minnesota at Duluth, Duluth MN 55812 (tel.: 218–726–8237; department office: 218–726–6370).

At the graduate level, all current member institutions of the Association of Graduate Liberal Studies Programs (AGLSP) have interdisciplinary cores. The AGLSP has produced several books on graduate liberal studies, including two collections of essays:

• Hands, Charles (ed.). *The Tradition in Modern Times*. Lanham, Md.: University Press of America, 1988.
• O'Callaghan, Phyllis (ed.). *A Clashing of Symbols*. Washington, D.C.: Georgetown University Press, 1988.

The AGLSP sells packets for program design and booklets of sample syllabi in the areas of historical, cultural, and science and technology studies. The current president is Diane Sasson, who can be reached at the Master of Arts in Liberal Studies Programs, 138 Social Sciences Building, Duke University, Durham NC 27708 (tel.: 919–684–3222). The presidency and institutional home change every two years. After 1996, the office at Duke will refer calls to the current president and institution.

Electronic Searching. Electronic on-line data bases offer great promise. In a recent study of journalism classes researching judicial decisions related to mass media, Bartolo and Smith found higher precision rates for on-line searching than for manual searching. Nevertheless, electronic searching is fraught with challenges. The problem of interdisciplinary information is the problem of information scattering. Appropriate materials do not appear in a single location, nor are they readily identified by cataloguing, indexing, and on-line services, which tend to mirror existing disciplinary categories. Hence, finding interdisciplinary information parallels the interdisciplinary process itself. Searchers must develop some expertise in moving across the varied assumptions, structures, and forms of disciplinary literatures as well as the invisible colleges, networks, and hybrid communities in which interdisciplinary knowledge often develops. As Fiscella emphasizes, searchers cannot simply apply a formula or routine but must make judgments throughout the searching process:

• Fiscella, Joan B. "Access to Interdisciplinary Information: Setting the Problem." *Issues in Integrative Studies*, 1989, 7, 73–92.

A literature on this subject has emerged in recent years. The reader will want to consult Fiscella (above) as well as the following works:

• Hurd, Julie. "Interdisciplinary Research in the Sciences: Implications for Library Organization." *College and Research Libraries*, July 1992, pp. 283–297.
• "Interdisciplinarity and Information: Issues and Access." *Issues in Integrative Studies*, 1992, 10 (special issue).
• Bartolo, L., and T. Smith. "Interdisciplinary Work and the Information Search Process: A Comparison of Manual and On-line Searching." *College and Research Libraries*, July 1993, pp. 344–353.

Of unique note, Issue no. 10 contains a discussion by Richard Carp about creating an interdisciplinary image bank, in this case an indexed set of slides for the teaching of world religion.

Some indexing services—for instance, *Pollution Abstracts and Environmental Bibliography*—serve particular interdisciplinary fields. However, interdisciplinary needs still outstrip current capacities. Using the sciences as an example, Hurd notes a number of solutions. Broader divisional science libraries are better than separate collections at supporting interdisciplinary needs. Science libraries operating in a decentralized environment can employ intracampus exchange programs to enable users to browse new journal issues or title pages. They can also use campus mail, couriers, and telefax transmission to deliver documents to and among dispersed sites. E-mail networks make it possible to communicate with remote libraries regarding reference questions, on-line search requests, book and journal delivery, and circulation and interlibrary loan services. Most of all, early and ongoing consultations with library staff are vital for materials acquisition and development of support services for interdisciplinary programs and research centers.

The results of any particular electronic search depend on when the search is performed, how recently the data base was updated, and the flexibility of the software system. Nevertheless, a universal caveat applies: without a carefully designed strategy, any yield may be overwhelming. A recent search of the ERIC data base using the keyword *interdisciplinary* yielded more than 12,500 citations. Using the descriptor *interdisciplinary approach* narrowed the yield slightly—to more than 10,000 items—while narrowing the search to material published only during the 1990s trimmed the count to 1,000. Joan Fiscella offers concrete advice for formulation of an appropriate search strategy either on your own or with the assistance of library personnel:

1. Define your beginning point, that is, what you know already. Take along models of what you are seeking, such as sample citations or copies of actual material.

2. Be as precise as possible about what you are and are not seeking. Specify whether you want subjects, methods, models, techniques, programs, pedagogy, theory, practice, examples, concepts, and/or research as well the appropriate level of education. Also indicate desired formats, such as articles, reports, books, proceedings, videotapes, slides, software, and/or optical discs.
3. Indicate how much you want—a comprehensive search or a broad sample? If uncertain, start out searching broadly until you find items that typify your needs. A search based on controlled vocabulary leads to a high degree of precision for a particular topic, but it may miss relevant items that the indexer has not included or that have different names in different data bases—a particular problem for interdisciplinary contexts. A free-text search will produce a high yield, but it requires culling relevant items from numerous citations.
4. Determine which literatures you want to search. Which disciplines, professional associations, organizations and personnel interest you most? Do you want to search scholarly, professional, and/or popular literatures?
5. Determine which terminology best expresses your needs. Are there alternative terms and concepts? Build a list of appropriate terms by checking subject areas in pertinent fields and consulting data base thesauri, which, again, differ from service to service and from discipline to discipline.
6. Define the desired time frame. Is it recent, historical, or both? If the yield proves too large, narrow the search by dates and educational levels.
7. Specify geographical and language considerations. Do you want to limit your search to the United States and to English-language works?

One of the most abundant data bases is the ERIC system. Items are listed in monthly issues of *Resources in Education* (*RIE*) and *Current Index to Journals in Education* (*CIJE*). The information in these journals can be searched by hand or by computer. Computerized searching has the added advantage of automatically including references listed in both *RIE* and *CIJE*. Items coded with an ED number are available on microfiche. Items coded with an EJ number refer to publications in journals. James Palmer has already identified a number of significant references:

• Palmer, James. "Interdisciplinary Studies: An ERIC Review." *Community College Review*, 1983, *11*(1), 59–64.

In addition, ERIC offers a service called AskERIC, an Internet-based question-answering service for teachers, administrators, and library personnel seeking information on K–12 education.

While ERIC is outstanding, it is not the only good source. Others include OCLC (a catalogue of materials, including audiovisual resources, held in libraries across the country), Current Contents (lists of tables of contents for major journals available in print or electronic version), and the various citation indexes (lists of publications in which authors have been cited). Subject- and field-specific indexes are also available in print and electronic versions. Print indexes include *Sociological Abstracts*, *Psychological Abstracts*, *American*

History and Life, *Philosopher's Index*, *MLA International Bibliography*, *Chemical Abstracts*, *Physics Abstracts*, *The Engineering Index*, and *Energy Information Abstracts*. The names of their electronic counterparts vary by vendor and format, so always check first with local library staff.

These days searchers can take advantage of new tools that facilitate access to the vast Internet system that connects campuses and other organizations electronically. Such tools as Gopher, Archie, WAIS, Worldwide Web, Veronica, and Jughead promote the finding and retrieval of data available on the Internet. (See Wilson, David. "Array of New Tools." *Chronicle of Higher Education*, May 26, 1993, pp. A17–A19.) For example, Veronica can be used to search the text of Gopher menus and retrieve information on interdisciplinary courses offered at the growing number of universities that have put course descriptions on-line. A recent search using *interdisciplinary* as a keyword yielded a number of citations and networking resources: course descriptions, bibliographies, announcements, and electronic conversations and discussion lists in the areas of play, games, and sports; natural resources, range management, and forest services; technology transfer and engineering; eighteenth-century studies, multiculturalism, and consciousness.

The main problem in using data base systems and tools is their escalating development. Keeping up with rapid changes in master indexes to vendor files, retrieval software, and technological advances is a challenge even for professionals. Again, the best place to start is with the personnel of your local library and computer center. Indexes and abstracts are available on CD-ROM and through local computer systems, often at little or no direct cost to the searcher. However, as government support declines, the private sector will play a larger role, and user fees are likely to grow. Nevertheless, a well-designed search strategy tapping local, regional, and national networks will reap benefits worth any cost.

The value of data base searching cannot be overstated. There are, for instance, literally thousands of books, articles, conference papers, speeches, reports, syllabi, case studies, program descriptions, and other less visible resources available through the ERIC system. Many of these items would be difficult or even impossible to locate through other means. For example, the first three numbers of *Issues in Integrative Studies*, which are now out of print, are available on ERIC fiche ED 268 015. The first issue contains Tom Benson's "Five Arguments Against Interdisciplinary Studies." A number of conference papers are also worthy of note:

- Salmon-Cox, Leslie, and Burkhart Holzner. "Managing Multidisciplinarity: Building and Bridging Epistemologies in Educational R&D." (ED 135 760)
- Assimopoulos, Nadia, and Belanger, Charles. "Interdisciplinary Policies and Practices." (ED 161 366)
- Becker, Samuel. "Innovations in Administration Used and Being Used by Other Departments." (ED 147 885)
- Kermoade, Arthur. "The Interdisciplinary Approach and Its Comparative Effectiveness." (ED 064 238)

- Connelly, Thomas. "Interdisciplinary References III: A Reference Document for Those Contemplating Interdisciplinary Education Programs in the Health Sciences." (ED 129 134)

Salmon-Cox and Holzner's 1977 paper, for a meeting of the American Education Research Association, examines conditions under which multidisciplinarity flourishes. The 1978 paper by Assimopoulos and Belanger, for the Association for Institutional Research Forum, covers students' responsiveness to course offerings outside their basic disciplines. Becker's 1977 paper, presented at a meeting of the Speech Communication Association, is rich in ideas for working cooperatively. Kermoade reports on a Seattle middle school project, and Connelly's work draws on the training programs of the Kentucky January Prototype at the Lexington College of Allied Health Professions.

Periodic searches of ERIC and other data bases are essential for staying on top of new material. So is cultivating a network of friends and professional peers who are willing to keep one another posted on new items, whether by phone, correspondence, or electronic mail. Electronic updating will always require some culling. For instance, using *interdisciplinary* as a keyword in ERIC will retrieve a multitude of irrelevant items on writing across the curriculum (WAC)—signalling the need to make WAC a separate category rather than conflating it with *interdisciplinary*. A recent search in ERIC turned up a variety of new and earlier items being updated in the data base:

- Astin, Paul. "Interdisciplinarity: Education for Social Consciousness." Opinion Paper Report. California, 1986. (ED 283 450)
- Indiana Governor's Scholars Academy. *Interdisciplinary Curriculum Outlines*. Indianapolis: Indiana Department of Education, Ball State University, 1990.
- Kowalewski, David, and Roy Laird. "Interdisciplinary Gaps: A Survey Report." *Educational Research Quarterly*, 1990, *14*(2), 32–40.
- Lounsberry, John H. *Connecting the Curriculum Through Interdisciplinary Instruction*. Columbus, Ohio: National Middle School Association, 1992.
- *Making Connections: Interdisciplinary Programs*. Harrisonburg, Pa.: James Madison University, 1991.
- *Perspectives on Interdisciplinary Education*. Golden Valley: Minnesota Center for Arts Education, 1992.

The Concept of Interdisciplinarity

The adjective *interdisciplinary* is the common label for a multitude of activities that extend beyond and enrich IDS. Foremost among them are tool and method borrowing, collaborative problem solving, complex research queries, transdisciplinary paradigms, cross-fertilizing concepts, interdisciplinary schools of thought, hybrid fields, and interdisciplines. Attempts to reach pertinent literatures always face the problem of information scattering. The best strategy is twofold: use core literatures as entry points, and network with specialized organizations.

There are three reliable points of entry into core literatures:
- Klein, Julie Thompson. *Interdisciplinarity: History, Theory, and Practice.* Detroit: Wayne State University Press, 1990.
- Klein, Julie Thompson. *Crossing Boundaries: Knowledge, Disciplinarities, and Interdisciplinarities.* Charlottesville: University Press of Virginia, forthcoming.
- Chubin, D. E., and others (eds.). *Interdisciplinary Analysis and Research: Theory and Practice of Problem-Focused Research and Development.* Mt. Airy, Md.: Lomond, 1986.

Klein (1990) offers a comprehensive synthesis of modern scholarship covering interdisciplinary research, education, and practice across the social and natural sciences, humanities, problem-focused research, health care, and education. The book also contains a ninety-four-page bibliography. Klein (forthcoming) focuses on current knowledge description and institutional practices, examines the link between interdisciplinarity and poststructuralist scholarship, interdisciplinary fields of knowledge, shifting definitions of interdisciplinarity in the discipline of literary studies, and new funding initiatives in science and technology. Chubin and colleagues offer an anthology of essays emphasizing problem-focused research. It contains an annotated bibliography and reprints such major pieces as Donald Campbell's "Ethnocentrism of Disciplines and the Fish Scale Model of Omniscience," Barmarck and Wallen's "The Interaction of Cognitive and Social Factors in Steering a Large Scale Interdisciplinary Project," Robert Chen's "Interdisciplinary Research and Integration: The Case of CO^2 and Climate," Darden and Maull's "Interfield Theories," Jacob Stucki's "A Goal-Oriented Pharmaceutical Research and Development Organization," Bella and Williamson's "Conflicts in Interdisciplinary Research," and Rossini and colleagues' "Interdisciplinary Integration within Technology Assessments."

Historically, two books have enjoyed the status of seminal works:
- Organization for Economic Cooperation and Development. *Interdisciplinarity: Problems of Teaching and Research in Universities.* Paris: OECD, 1972.
- Kockelmans, Joseph J. (ed.). *Interdisciplinarity and Higher Education.* University Park: Pennsylvania State University Press, 1979.

For almost two decades, the 1972 OECD volume was the most widely cited publication on interdisciplinarity. This pioneer study is dominated by the structuralist and general systems thinking of its major theorists, among them Jean Piaget, Leo Apostel, Guy Berger, and Erich Jantsch. The book, which responded to worldwide demands for reform, contains a typology of interdisciplinary activities and definitions of the relationship between disciplinarity and interdisciplinarity. Twelve years later, when the OECD returned to the subject of interdisciplinarity at the international meeting that produced *Interdisciplinarity Revisited*, cited earlier, the optimism of the 1970s had been replaced by the empirical realism of the 1980s. Financial cutbacks had hit universities worldwide, and interdisciplinarians were testing their theories in the forge of daily practice.

In the United States, Kockelmans' work has enjoyed a comparable level of influence. This collection of papers from a postgraduate seminar situates the earlier OECD book in the U.S. context. Joseph Kockelmans, Hans Flexner, and Wolfram Swoboda analyze the historical relationship between disciplinarity and interdisciplinarity. The volume also includes Rustum Roy's oft-quoted analysis of materials science and Jonathan Broido's lengthy assessment of interdisciplinary methodology, with critical appraisals of structuralism, unity of science, and system theory as interdisciplinary approaches. Two earlier works are in the vein of the Kockelmans collection:

- Gusdorf, George. "Past, Present, and Future in Interdisciplinary Research," *International Social Science Journal*, 1977, 29(4), 580–599.
- Delkeskamp, Corinna. "Interdisciplinarity: A Critical Appraisal." In H. T. Engelhardt, Jr., and D. Callahan (eds.), *Knowledge, Value, and Belief.* Hastings-on-Hudson, N.Y.: Hastings Center, 1977.

Gusdorf reflects historically on interdisciplinary research, while Delkeskamp weighs the epistemological and social claims of interdisciplinarity.

Recently, Fuller has advanced a rhetorical conception of interdisciplinary theory and process:

- Fuller, Steve. "The Position: Interdisciplinarity as Interpenetration." In *Philosophy, Rhetoric, and the End of Knowledge: The Coming of Science and Technology Studies.* Madison: University of Wisconsin Press, 1993.

Excerpts from a Smithsonian Seminar Series on "Knowledge Collaborations in the Arts, the Sciences and the Humanities" offer an overview of recent collaborative and interdisciplinary work. They are available over several journal issues of *Knowledge: Creation, Diffusion, Utilization*:

- Part I: "The Arts," 1991, 13(2), 193–215.
- Part II: "The Sciences," 1992, 13(4), 399–409.
- Part III: "The Humanities and Social Sciences," 1992, 14(1), 110–132.
- Part IV: "Collaboration, for Better or for Worse," 1992, 14(1), 133–142.

Much of the best scholarship on interdisciplinarity is not global or theoretical in a general way but regional and local, that is, focused on particular interdisciplinary fields, specific clusters of disciplinary relations, and interdisciplinary activities and traditions within individual disciplines. The literatures on education and the social sciences experienced the first large growth in these areas, followed by the literatures on problem-focused research, health care, and alliances between the humanities and the social and natural sciences and technology. In the past decade, expanding sociological studies of knowledge and studies of disciplinarity have made disciplinary literatures increasingly fruitful sites for information on interdisciplinary developments. This trend reflects the growing belief that knowledge is increasingly interdisciplinary. Five recent publications provide a sense of this discussion:

- Association of American Colleges and Universities. *Liberal Learning and the*

Arts and Sciences Major. Vol. 1: *The Challenge of Connecting Learning.* Washington, D.C.: AACU, 1990
- Vol. 2: *Reports from the Fields.* Washington, D.C.: AACU, 1990.
- Vol. 3: *Program Review and Educational Quality in the Major.* Washington, D.C.: AACU, 1991.
- Easton, David, and Corinne Schelling (eds.). *Divided Knowledge: Across Disciplines, Across Fields.* Newbury Park, Calif.: Sage, 1991.
- Messer-Davidow, E., D. Shumway, and D. Sylvan (eds.). *Knowledges: Historical and Critical Studies of Disciplinarity.* Charlottesville: University Press of Virginia, 1993.

Easton and Schelling's work contains reports on recent trends in the social sciences and humanities. *Knowledges* is the lead volume in a new series called *Knowledge: Disciplinarity and Beyond.*

One excellent way of learning about new reports, studies, and books on the state of a discipline, new research trends, and interdisciplinary subfields is to monitor the journals and newsletters published by major learned societies. Sessions on the state of the discipline and on new research at the annual meetings of professional associations are another good place to learn about bibliography. Book reviews that survey a particular theme, problem, or subfield are yet another good source. Discipline-specific journals with a teaching orientation, such as *History Teacher*, and journals with a general orientation, such as *Science and Synthesis*, are other excellent sites to monitor. The more fully organizations employ the strategies recommended in Chapter Five of this volume, the better served their individual members will be. Individuals working on their own will find organizational newsletters and news columns in journals especially helpful. Illustrating their value, Susan Searing (1992) reports that a recent survey of women's studies researchers showed a surprising reliance on newsletters of women's organizations as sources of information. However, action-oriented publications are rarely found in academic libraries. In addition to these strategies, a number of published works provide fruitful entry points for specialized needs.

The Social Sciences. Interdisciplinarity has a long and rich history in the social sciences, as evidenced by periodic reports on interdisciplinary research in the journal *Social Science Information* and special sections of the *International Social Science Journal*, including:
- "Multidisciplinary Problem-Focused Research." *International Social Science Journal*, 1968, 20(2).
- "Facets of Interdisciplinarity." *International Social Science Journal*, 1977, 29(4).

Three overviews provide an excellent introduction:
- Landau, M., H. Proshansky, and W. Ittelson. "The Interdisciplinary Approach and the Concept of Behavioral Sciences." In Norman F. Washburne (ed.), *Decisions, Values and Groups.* New York: Pergamon Press, 1962.

- Miller, Raymond C. "Varieties of Interdisciplinary Approaches in the Social Sciences." *Issues in Integrative Studies*, 1982, *1*, 1–37.
- Dogan, Mattei, and Robert Pahre. *Creative Marginality: Innovation at the Intersections of the Social Sciences*. Boulder, Colo.: Westview Press, 1990.

Landau, Proshansky, and Ittelson trace two distinct interdisciplinary movements in the social sciences, Miller presents a classification scheme, while Dogan and Pahre examine innovation and originality at the borders of disciplines.

The older core works on interdisciplinary social sciences include a collection of essays:

- Sherif, Muzafer, and Carolyn Sherif (eds.). *Interdisciplinary Relationships in the Social Sciences*. Chicago: Aldine, 1969.

This book is the original source of Donald Campbell's oft-cited "Ethnocentrism of Disciplines and the Fish-Scale Model of Omniscience." It also contains Marvin Mikesell's "The Borderlands of Geography as a Social Science, the Sherifs' "Interdisciplinary Coordination as a Validity Check: Retrospect and Prospects," and Robert Dubin's "Contiguous Problem Analysis: An Approach to Systematic Theories about Social Organization." Readers should also take note of a book by Phillips, who saw three distinguishable theses about complex entities in holism, as well as a rejoinder by Bailis:

- Phillips, D. C. *Holistic Thought in the Social Sciences*. Stanford, Calif.: Stanford University Press, 1976.
- Bailis, Stanley. "Against and for Holism: A Review and Rejoinder to D. C. Phillips." *Issues in Integrative Studies*, 1984–1985, *3*, 17–41.

No list would be complete without certain perennial favorites on interdisciplinary syllabi:

- Eisely, Loren. *The Immense Journey*. New York: Random House, 1956.
- Boulding, Kenneth. *The Image: Knowledge in Life and Society*. Ann Arbor: University of Michigan Press, 1956.
- Bateson, Gregory. *Mind and Nature: A Necessary Unity*. New York: Dutton, 1979.
- Bellah, Robert, and others. *Habits of the Heart: Individualism and Commitment in American Life*. New York: Knopf, 1982.
- Hofstadter, Douglas. *Gödel, Escher, Bach: An Eternal Golden Braid*. New York: Basic Books, 1979.

Eisely has long been a favorite because of the skill with which he combines anthropological knowledge with literary imagination in a passage through time. Drawing on biology, psychology, sociology, political science, economics, and history to make a classic case for integrated knowledge, Boulding proposes a new interdisciplinary science of "eiconics." Bateson views biological evolution as a paradigm for understanding processes of thought, cultural change, and education. Two more recent items have begun to appear on syllabi: Bellah and colleagues' work makes rich use of the interview as an interdisciplinary tool. Hofstadter bridges the sciences and humanities in developing the idea that reality is a system of interconnecting and interrelating braids.

Contemporary scholarship focuses on a variety of topics, ranging from alliances between older disciplines to postmodern boundary crossing. The monitoring strategies described earlier in this chapter can be used to locate discipline-specific analyses. Two recent publications deserve special notice:

- Fisher, Donald. *Fundamental Development of the Social Sciences*. Ann Arbor: University of Michigan Press, 1993.
- Calhoun, Craig. "Sociology, Other Disciplines, and the Project of a General Understanding of Social Life." In Terence Halliday and Morris Janowitz (eds.), *Sociology and Its Publics*. Chicago: University of Chicago Press, 1992, pp. 137-95.

Fisher analyzes the boundary work of the Social Science Research Council, a major organization in interdisciplinary history. Calhoun, who analyzes sociology's historical and contemporary relations with other social sciences, provides a wide review of interdisciplinary trends and interests.

Three decades ago the most influential contributions to interdisciplinary theory came from the social sciences. Today, they are emerging from the intersections between the humanities and the social sciences. The influence of the thinkers discussed in Skinner's edited collection is widely and strongly felt:

- Skinner, Quentin (ed.). *The Return of Grand Theory in the Human Sciences*. Cambridge, England: Cambridge University Press, 1985.

Skinner concedes that his title may be ironic, since the book's subjects— Gadamer, Derrida, Foucault, Kuhn, Habermas, Althusser, Lévi-Strauss, and the *Annales* historians—have differing and in some cases highly skeptical views of social theory.

Anthropology has been an especially intense zone of cross-fertilization. For many, the seminal reference is an essay by Geertz, who examines analogies drawn from the humanities:

- Geertz, Clifford. "Blurred Genres: The Refiguration of Social Thought." *American Scholar*, 1980, 49(2), 165–179. Reprinted in Clifford Geertz, *Local Knowledge: Further Essays in Interpretive Anthropology*. New York: Basic Books, 1983.

These analogies—game, drama, text, speech-act analysis, discourse, and representationalist approaches related to cognitive aesthetics—have played an increasingly visible role in sociological and anthropological explanation. Other entry points include:

- Clifford, James, and George Marcus (eds.). *Writing Culture: The Poetics and Politics of Ethnography*. Berkeley: University of California Press, 1986.
- Fox, Richard D. (ed.). *Recapturing Anthropology: Working in the Present*. Santa Fe, N.M.: School of American Research Press, 1991.

The Humanities. In conceptualizing the interdisciplinary humanities, teachers and administrators might begin with Cluck's work:

- Cluck, Nancy Anne. "Reflections on the Interdisciplinary Approaches to the Humanities." *Liberal Education*, Spring 1980, pp. 67–77.

Building on R. S. Crane's suggestion that four groups of skills are central to the humanities, Cluck proposes that historical periods, ideas, aesthetic themes, and structures furnish junctures that can serve as common ground among humanities disciplines. The following works provide other reliable entry points into these cross-fertilizations:

- Casey, Beth. "The Quiet Revolution: The Transformation and Reintegration of the Humanities." *Issues in Integrative Studies*, 1986, 4, 71–92.
- Nelson, J. S., A. Megill, and D. N. McCloskey (eds.). *The Rhetoric of the Human Sciences: Language and Argument in Scholarship and Public Affairs.* Madison: University of Wisconsin Press, 1987.
- Simons, Herbert W. (ed.). *Rhetoric in the Human Sciences.* London: Sage, 1989.
- Simons, Herbert W. (ed.). *The Rhetorical Turn: Invention and Persuasion in the Conduct of Inquiry.* Chicago: University of Chicago Press, 1990.

Casey provides a good introduction to the relationship among interdisciplinarity, postmodernism, and the humanities. She is especially mindful of activities that scholarship has labeled the *rhetorical, interpretive,* and *linguistic turns.*

The humanities have long been an integrative force in the curriculum. This tradition is especially strong in alternatives to traditional models of general education, the fastest-growing sector of interdisciplinary studies today. Many of the items mentioned in the earlier section on *Published Collections* and many articles dealing with core curriculum have a strong humanities emphasis. Additionally, the ERIC data base has a number of resources on the teaching of humanities. For example, a recent search netted "Bridges and Boundaries"; three more widely available works also aid in curriculum development:

- "Bridges and Boundaries in the Humanities, Arts, and Social Sciences." New York: Columbia University, 1982. (Available in *Proceedings, General Education Seminar,* 9, 1980–1981.)
- Foa, Lin. "The Integrated Humanities in Higher Education: A Survey." *Journal of Aesthetic Education*, 1973, 7, 85–98.
- Crandall, Deborah, and Elizabeth Rinnander. "Interdisciplinary Humanities: Sources and Information." In Leslie Koltai (ed.), *Merging the Humanities.* New Directions for Community Colleges, no. 12. San Francisco: Jossey-Bass, 1975.
- Brooks, Anne, and Un-chol Shin. "Past, Present, and Future of Interdisciplinary Humanities." *Humanities Education*, September 1984, pp. 3–9.

Finding reliable entry points is as crucial here as it is in the social sciences. To take literary studies as an example, two works provide overviews:

- Gunn, Giles. "Interdisciplinary Studies." In Joseph Gibaldi (ed.), *Introduction to Scholarship in Modern Languages and Literatures* (2nd ed.). New York: Modern Language Association, 1992.

- Klein, Julie Thompson. "Interdisciplinary Genealogy in Literary Studies." In *Crossing Boundaries: Knowledge, Disciplinarities, and Interdisciplinarities.* Charlottesville: University Press of Virginia, forthcoming.

Gunn focuses on contemporary activity, while Klein's chapter focuses on professional guides and histories. Both sources lead to other pertinent literature:

- Fish, Stanley. "Being Interdisciplinary Is So Very Hard to Do." In *Profession 89.* New York: Modern Language Association, 1989.
- Greenblatt, Stephen, and Giles Gunn (eds.). *Redrawing the Boundaries.* New York: Modern Language Association, 1992.
- Barricelli, J.-P., J. Gibaldi, and E. Lauter (eds.). *Teaching Literature and the Other Arts.* New York: Modern Language Association, 1990.

The fact that the Modern Language Association has published extensive resources for interdisciplinary curricula, including Barricelli, Gibaldi, and Lauter, underscores the importance of networking through professional organizations.

In art history, a profusion of interdisciplinary, postmodern, and multicultural interests has generated a sizable literature on boundary crossing, including:

- Kraft, Selma. "Interdisciplinarity and the Canon of Art History." *Issues in Integrative Studies,* 1989, 7, 57–71.
- Stafford, Barbara M. "The Eighteenth Century: Towards an Interdisciplinary Model." *Art Bulletin,* 1988, 70(1), 6–24.
- Bal, Mieke. *Reading "Rembrandt": Beyond the Word-Image Opposition.* Cambridge, England: Cambridge University Press, 1991.

Kraft introduces the subject, and, in a bibliographically rich analysis, Stafford explores the problem of humanistic theory and specialist theory, while considering how links might be established between dissimilarly evolving disciplines and similar themes that go beyond eclecticism, reductionism, appropriation, and analogy. In an exemplary model of interdisciplinary scholarship, Bal explores the potential for interdisciplinary methodology constituted by visual textuality.

The debate on whether history is one of the humanities or a social science has long been a point of interdisciplinary discourse:

- Horn, T. C., and Harry Ritter. "Interdisciplinary History: A Historiographical Review." *History Teacher,* 1986, 19(3), 427–448.
- Burke, Peter (ed.). *New Perspectives on Historical Writing.* University Park: Pennsylvania University Press, 1991.
- Hareven, Tamara. "The History of the Family as an Interdisciplinary Field." *Journal of Interdisciplinary History,* 1971, 2(2), 339–441.

Horn and Ritter provide an excellent introduction. Burke's state-of-the-discipline book illuminates the dynamics of interdisciplinary work. Hareven provides keen insight into the dynamics of interdisciplinary research. Over the years, special issues of journals have also been fruitful sites of debate on particular junctures:

- *Social Science Quarterly,* 1969, *50*(1) (special issue).
- *Historical Methods,* 1986, *19*(3) (special section).
- *Social Science History,* 1987, *11*(1) (special section).

Social Science Quarterly addresses convergences in history and sociology, *Historical Methods* presents a dialogue on history and anthropology, while *Social Science History* contains a debate on historical sociology and social history.

A beginning reading list should also include the prologue, introduction, and epilogue to Hershberg:

- Hershberg, Theodore (ed.). *Philadelphia: Work, Space, Family, and Group Experience in the Nineteenth Century; Essays Toward an Interdisciplinary History of the City.* New York: Oxford University Press, 1981.

The Sciences and Technology. Strains of discussion in the interdisciplinary sciences and technology range from the cosmological to the instrumental, from ethics, holism, and the literature and science movement to macromolecular research and advanced technological breakthroughs. Two works are worth noting:

- Bechtel, William. "The Nature of Scientific Integration." In William Bechtel (ed.), *Integrating Scientific Disciplines.* Dordrecht, Netherlands: Martinus Nijhoff, 1986.
- Darden, Lindley, and Nancy Maull. "Interfield Theories." *Philosophy of Science,* 1977, *44,* 43–64. Also available in Chubin and others (1986).

Bechtel is a solid place to begin. The book covers biochemistry, the evolutionary synthesis, cognitive science, and animal ethology. In what has become a classic essay, Darden and Maull illustrate a major dimension of scientific integration by focusing on the chromosome theory of Mendelian heredity, operon theory, and allosteric regulation as it connected the fields of biochemistry and physical chemistry. These theories have played an important role in the progressive unification of the modern physical and biological sciences.

Results of a 1977 conference on the unity of the sciences reflect a different perspective:

- *The Search for Absolute Values in a Changing World.* 2 vols. New York: International Cultural Foundation, 1978.

Key works on holistic thought include:

- Radnitzky, Gerald (ed.). *Continental Schools of Metascience.* 2 vols. Goteborg, Sweden: Akademiforlaget, 1968.
- Odum, Eugene P. "The Emergence of Ecology as an Integrative Discipline." *Science,* 1977, *195,* 1289–1293.
- Bohm, David. *Wholeness and the Implicate Order.* London: Routledge & Kegan Paul, 1980.

In addition, Toulmin has collected essays dealing with the cosmological significance of the modern scientific world picture, with assessments of the work

of Arthur Koestler, Jacques Monod, Gregory Bateson, Carl Sagan, and Teilhard de Chardin:
- Toulmin, Stephen. *The Return to Cosmology: Postmodern Science and the Theology of Nature*. Berkeley: University of California Press, 1982.

One of the most rapidly growing areas of the curriculum is studies of science, technology, and society:
- Cutcliffe, Stephen. "Science, Technology, and Society." *National Forum*, 1989, 69(2), 22–25.
- Bazan, Gene. "Deep STS: Newsletters That Help." *STS Today*, May 1993, pp. 3, 4, 8, 10.
- Caldwell, Lynton. "Environmental Studies: Discipline or Metadiscipline?" *Environmental Professional*, 1983, 5, 247–259.
- Regier, Henry A. *A Balanced Science of Renewable Resources, with Particular Reference to Fisheries*. Seattle: Washington Sea Grant, University of Washington Press, 1978.
- Dahlberg, Kenneth A., and John W. Bennett. *Natural Resources and People: Conceptual Issues in Interdisciplinary Research*. Boulder, Colo.: Westview, 1986.
- Fuller, Steve. "The Position: Interdisciplinarity as Interpenetration." In *Philosophy, Rhetoric, and the End of Knowledge: The Coming of Science and Technology Studies*. Madison: University of Wisconsin Press, 1993.

Cutcliffe's essay provides an introduction to the subject. Illustrating the importance of monitoring newsletters, Bazan presents an annotated list of newsletters that deal with science and technology themes and issues. In a related area, Caldwell analyzes the nature and prospects of environmental studies. Regier considers the challenge of renewable resources from a research perspective. Multi- and interdisciplinary work is also a recurring theme in Dahlberg and Bennett's work. And, as noted earlier, Fuller's recent book on science and technology studies contains an important addition to the core literature on interdisciplinarity.

Interdisciplinary research is so widespread today that interdisciplinarity is often said to be the characterizing trait of contemporary science. Recent national reports provide overviews of basic and applied research framed by ongoing debate on the funding priorities for science and technology. To take the discipline of physics as an example, in the areas of polymers and complex fluids, condensed-matter physicists have become so concerned with problems involving macromolecular systems that the traditional boundaries between chemistry, physics, and even biology have blurred. New technologies and such sophisticated physical methods as high-speed electronics, optical communications, advanced medical instrumentation, exotic defense systems, and energy and environmental systems have "nucleated" and grown to maturity within a few years of the discoveries on which they are based. Simultaneously, ideas and methods born at the interfaces between sciences have increased the ability of researchers to address complex problems. In the realm of fundamental science, the most vigorous interdisciplinary interactions are in biophysics, materials science, the chemistry–physics interface, geophysics, and mathematical and computational physics. In technical applications of physics, which are pivotal to large-scale industrial technology, the outstanding examples involve electronics, optical information technologies, and the new instrumentation now being used in the fields of energy and environment, national security, and medicine. See especially:

- *Physics Through the 1990s*. Vol. 8: *Scientific Interfaces and Technological Applications*. Washington, D.C.: National Academy Press, 1990.
- Sigma Xi. *Removing the Boundaries: Perspectives on Cross-Disciplinary Research*. New Haven, Conn.: Sigma Xi, 1988.
- Sproull, Robert, and Harold Hall. *Multidisciplinary Research and Education Programs in Universities*. Washington, D.C.: Government-University-Industrial Research Roundtable, 1987.
- National Research Council. *Interdisciplinary Research: Promoting Collaboration Between the Life Sciences and Medicine and the Physical Sciences and Engineering*. Washington, D.C.: National Academy Press, 1990.

Interdisciplinary Fields

One key in the search for resources lies in knowing which journals are user-friendly to interdisciplinarians. Three journals are exemplary in this regard. *Signs: The Journal of Women in Culture and Society* publishes updates on pertinent scholarship on and about women in a variety of disciplines. The *Journal of Interdisciplinary History* analyzes and reviews subfields and trends in interdisciplinary history. *American Quarterly* publishes coded bibliography in the disciplines contributing to scholarship in American studies. Unfortunately, many of the best field-specific analyses are underidentified and thus underused. The following examples all belong in the core literature on interdisciplinarity:

- Binder, Arnold. (1987). "Criminology: Discipline or Interdiscipline?," *Issues in Integrative Studies*, 1987, 5, 41–68.
- "*Germanistik* as German Studies: Interdisciplinary Theories and Methods." *German Quarterly*, 1989, 62(2) (special issue).
- Grele, Ronald. "A Surmisable Variety: Interdisciplinarity and Oral Testimony." *American Quarterly*, August 1975, pp. 275–295.
- Hall, Stuart. "Cultural Studies and the Center: Some Problematics and Problems." In Stuart Hall and others (eds.), *Culture, Media, Language: Working Papers in Cultural Studies, 1972–79*. London: Hutchinson, 1984.
- Kroker, Arthur. "Migration Across the Disciplines." *Journal of Canadian Studies*, 1980, 15, 3–10.
- Lambert, Richard D. "Blurring the Disciplinary Boundaries: Area Studies in the United States." In David Easton and Corinne Schelling (eds.), *Divided Knowledge: Across Disciplines, Across Fields*. Newbury Park, Calif.: Sage, 1991.
- Lebow, R. N. "Interdisciplinary Research and the Future of Peace and Security Studies." *Political Psychology*, 1988, 9(3), 507–525.

- Rich, Daniel, and Robert Warren. "The Intellectual Future of Urban Affairs: Theoretical, Normative, and Organizational Options." *Social Science Journal*, 1980, *17*(2), 53–66.
- Stoddard, Ellwyn. "Multidisciplinary Research Funding: A 'Catch 22' Enigma." *American Sociologist*, November 1982, pp. 210–216.

A chapter by Pye and a double issue of *Social Science Journal* focused on borderlands studies are also of interest:

- Pye, Lucian. "The Confrontation Between Discipline and Area Studies." In Lucian Pye (ed.), *Political Science and Area Studies: Rivals or Partners?* Bloomington: Indiana University Press, 1975.
- *Social Science Journal*, 1975–1976, *1-112* (special issue).

Few teachers and administrators would ordinarily consider checking the literatures on interdisciplinary problem-focused research (IDR) and health care. However, this added step is well worth the time, especially for those interested in teamwork and problem solving. IDR is linked with the history of mission-oriented research and growing alliances among universities, government, and industry. Chubin and his co-authors date the origin of a literature on the subject to a 1951 paper, which examined the problems of collaboration between an anthropologist and a psychiatrist:

- Caudill, W., and B. H. Roberts. "Pitfalls in the Organization of Interdisciplinary Research." *Human Organization*, 1951, *10*, 12–15.

Two works provide an introduction to the subject:

- Bie, Pierre de. Introduction to "Multidisciplinary Problem-Focused Research" (special section). *International Social Science Journal*, 1968, *20*(2), 192–210.
- Klein, Julie T. "The Evolution of a Body of Knowledge: Interdisciplinary Problem-Focused Research." *Knowledge: Creation, Utilization, and Diffusion*, 1985, *7*(2), 117–142.

Bie's introduction defines the nature of problem-focused research in its multi- and interdisciplinary dimensions. Klein provides an introductory synthesis of scholarship on IDR (her 1990 work updates this earlier piece). Finally, to recall, the anthology by Chubin and others contains major reprints and an annotated bibliography with an emphasis on IDR.

IDR has also been the subject of six major books and special issues of several journals. Periodic international meetings of the International Association for the Study of Interdisciplinary Research (INTERSTUDY) resulted in the publication of four of these books and a special issue of the journal *R&D Management* (April 1984, vol. 14, no.2). *SRA, Journal of the Society of Research Administrators* did a special issue on management of interdisciplinary research (Fall 1981), and *Technological Forecasting and Social Change* dealt with problem-focused research (1979, vol. 2).

The first two INTERSTUDY books provide overviews:

- Barth, Richard T., and Rudy Steck (eds.). *Interdisciplinary Research Groups:*

Their Management and Organization. Vancouver: Interdisciplinary Research Group on Interdisciplinary Programs, 1979.

- Epton, S. R., R. L. Payne, and R. W. Pearson (eds.). *Managing Interdisciplinary Research.* Chichester, Great Britain: John Wiley, 1983.

Barth and Steck survey management, organizational structure, and group dynamics of IDR. Case studies are drawn from the pharmaceutical and telecommunication industries, technology assessments, a forest ecosystem project, an urban traffic system project, and work based in U.S., British, and Polish universities. In Epton, Payne, and Pearson, an introductory synthesis of nomenclature, concepts, and organizational forms is accompanied by essays on peer review, performance, productivity, and leadership. The case studies include projects on noise control, freshwater diversion, and marine technology; other case studies are drawn from the fields of biomedical sciences, genetic engineering, and futures research. The third and fourth INTERSTUDY books on IDR reflect more focused inquiries:

- Mar, B. W., W. T. Newell, and B. O. Saxberg (eds.). *Managing High Technology: An Interdisciplinary Perspective.* Amsterdam: North Holland, 1985.
- Birnbaum, P. H., F. A. Rossini, and D. R. Baldwin (eds.). *International Research Management: Studies in Interdisciplinary Methods from Business, Government, and Academia.* New York: Oxford University Press, 1990.

Mar, Newell, and Saxberg emphasize IDR in high technology settings. The case studies draw from pharmaceutics, electronics, space engineering, environmental assessment, technology forecasting, university engineering centers, and projects based in governmental settings and industrial R&D units. Increased representation from industry can be felt in the sustained focus on improving collaboration across academic disciplines in universities and functional activities in industry. The volume also contains papers on organizational forms and management strategies plus reflections on sociological and philosophical issues. Birnbaum, Rossini, and Baldwin's book focuses on the life cycle of IDR, covering preconditions, processes, and impacts. The case studies are drawn from Brazilian, Japanese, Israeli, and U.S. settings. The book also contains a sizable bibliography.

There are two other major works on IDR:

- Luszki, Margaret Barron. *Interdisciplinary Team Research: Methods and Problems.* New York: New York University Press, 1958.
- Russell, M. G., J. M. Barnes, and J. R. Cornwell (eds.). *Enabling Interdisciplinary Research: Perspectives from Agriculture, Forestry, and Home Economics.* Miscellaneous Publications 19. St. Paul: Agricultural Experiment Station, University of Minnesota, 1982.

In a sustained analysis of interdisciplinary teamwork, Luszki examines the relationships among psychologists, psychiatrists, and sociologists working on mental health projects. Based in the land grant tradition, mission orientation, and system of state experiment stations sponsored by the United States Department of Agriculture, the collection edited by Russell, Barnes, and Cornwell accounts for an important chapter in the history of IDR. Interdisciplinary work in agriculture, plant sciences, forestry, animal sciences, family studies, and home economics conducted under these auspices represents a rich store of knowledge on interdisciplinary collaborative research and problem solving.

The literatures on IDR and health care further illuminate the dynamics of interdisciplinary teamwork. Notable references include:

- MacDonald, William. "The Characteristics of Interdisciplinary Research Teams." In D. E. Chubin and others (eds.). *Interdisciplinary Analysis and Research: Theory and Practice of Problem-Focused Research and Development.* Mt. Airy, Md.: Lomond, 1986.
- Stone, Anthony. "The Interdisciplinary Research Team." *Journal of Applied Behavioral Science,* 1969, 5, 351–365.
- McCorcle, Mitchell. "Critical Issues in the Functioning of Interdisciplinary Groups." *Small Group Behavior,* 1982, 13, 291–310.

Stone analyzed interdisciplinary teams as interacting task-oriented groups that form two ideal types, primary and secondary groups. Successful teamwork depends on a shift from secondary-group relations, which are protective of the individual, to primary-group relations, which are dedicated to a common task and a shared cognitive framework.

Four additional publications deserve mention:

- Ducanis, Alex J., and Anne K. Golin. *The Interdisciplinary Health Care Team: A Handbook.* Germantown: Aspen Systems Corp., 1979.
- Day, Donald W. "Perspectives on Care: The Interdisciplinary Team Ap-proach." *Otolaryngologic Clinics of North America,* 1981, 14(4), 769–775.
- Morris, Hughlett L. "The Structure and Function of Interdisciplinary Health Teams." In Carlos F. Salinas and Ronald J. Jorgenson (eds.), *Dentistry in the Interdisciplinary Treatment of Genetic Disease.* New York: Alan R. Liss, 1980.
- Turner, Brian. "The Interdisciplinary Curriculum: From Social Medicine to Postmodernism." *Sociology of Health and Illness,* 1990, 12(1), 1–23.

The first three references deal pragmatically with teamwork issues. Turner's piece is oriented toward larger issues and represents a significant new addition to the core literature on interdisciplinarity.

Interdisciplinarity, Turner explains, emerged as an epistemological goal as the result of the focus in the fields of social medicine and sociology of health on the complex causality of illness and disease and on the notion that any valid therapeutic must be based on a holistic view of the patient. Turner contrasts interdisciplinarity in this sense with the interdisciplinary research centers organized in the United Kingdom under the Thatcher government. Based on teamwork supported by private and public sector funding, these centers are an unintended consequence of economic necessity, not scientific theory. Like their counterparts in the United States, they have tended to produce ad hoc, short-term alliances and coalitions between sectors. Moreover, while postmodern social theory challenges monodisciplinarity, the current commercialization of medicine, when combined with postmodern criticism of the conventional medical curriculum, may well result in increased fragmentation, not in intellectual integration.

Turner's analysis returns us to two interdisciplinary realities. First, the current diversity of interdisciplinary practices has generated a voluminous literature. Second, these practices produce information needs that differ dramatically from those of twenty years ago, and the divergence will only increase. At present, we are in an interim state. Interdisciplinary fields call into question the very verbal, numerical, and spatial systems on which we must rely:

- Searing, Susan E. "How Librarians Cope with Interdisciplinarity: The Case of Women's Studies." *Issues in Integrative Studies*, 1992, 10, 7.

Well-honed strategies are our best hope for finding the knowledge and information that we must have in order to respond, to teach, and to administer.

JULIE THOMPSON KLEIN, professor of humanities at Wayne State University, has been visiting foreign professor at Shimane University in Japan and senior Fulbright lecturer and academic specialist in democracy in Nepal. She often consults on interdisciplinary programs and institutional change.

This step-by-step guide to the design of interdisciplinary courses explores their underlying theoretical rationales and expected educational outcomes while offering concrete suggestions and examples for every step of the course design and instruction process.

Designing Interdisciplinary Courses

William H. Newell

Interdisciplinary courses promise a wide range of desirable educational outcomes for students. Students in high-quality interdisciplinary courses are consistently reported to develop the traditional liberal arts skills of precision and clarity in reading, writing, speaking, and thinking; to confront challenges to their assumptions about themselves and their world; and to develop the habit of asking why instead of merely memorizing accepted facts. The student-centered ambiance of many interdisciplinary programs seems to promote mutual respect between students and faculty and among students of diverse backgrounds; it also leads to the development of affective as well as cognitive skills (Newell and Davis, 1988). These outcomes stem as much from the way in which the courses are taught as they do from their interdisciplinary nature.

Other educational outcomes seem to be a product of the interdisciplinary process itself: an appreciation for perspectives other than one's own; an ability to evaluate the testimony of experts; tolerance of ambiguity; increased sensitivity to ethical issues; an ability to synthesize or integrate; enlarged perspectives or horizons; more creative, original, or unconventional thinking; increased humility or listening skills; and sensitivity to disciplinary, political, or religious bias (Davis and Newell, 1981).

Interdisciplinary courses have advantages for institutions as well. Since topically focused interdisciplinary courses are inherently more interesting to take and teach than introductory or survey courses, they improve morale in required general education courses. They can also serve as efficient introductions to the various disciplines (Newell, 1983a). They offer a relatively low-cost but highly effective form of faculty development that facilitates reallocation of fixed faculty costs from underenrolled departments (Armstrong, 1980).

NEW DIRECTIONS FOR TEACHING AND LEARNING, no. 58, Summer 1994 © Jossey-Bass Publishers

Half a dozen years ago, a comprehensive study of American undergraduate interdisciplinary programs (Newell, 1988) showed that institutions had responded to the manifold promise of interdisciplinarity by developing, first, new institutionwide general education programs in which interdisciplinary components were required and, second, interdisciplinary honors, humanities, and women's studies programs. These programs were at once surprisingly numerous, geographically dispersed, large, egalitarian, and recent in origin. Indeed, more than half of the programs documented in the study had been formed within the preceding dozen years. These developments have moved interdisciplinary study from the radical fringe to the liberal mainstream. Such reform, which builds on disciplines instead of supplanting them, has taken place in the name of excellence as well as coherence, although sometimes it has had a critical edge. Since the study cited, undergraduate interdisciplinarity seems to have accelerated even more, with almost all the growth coming in general education. For example, state boards of regents and councils of higher education now tend to see distributive general education as outmoded, and interdisciplinary approaches as the innovative norm (Miller and McCartan, 1990).

This chapter focuses on the process of designing an undergraduate interdisciplinary course. The process has eight steps: assembling an interdisciplinary team, selecting the topic, identifying disciplines, developing the subtext, structuring the course, selecting readings, designing assignments, and preparing the syllabus. Given the curricular context just discussed, most of the examples in this chapter have been drawn from interdisciplinary general education, although the focus is still broad enough to include interdisciplinary courses in honors, humanities, and women's studies as well as courses sometimes found in adult education; American studies; environmental studies; ethnic studies; science, technology, values, and society; the social and natural sciences; urban studies; global studies—and in some disciplinary departments (Newell, 1986).

Assembling an Interdisciplinary Team

Interdisciplinary teams have four common uses in teaching: for course development (our focus here as the first step in the course design process), faculty development seminars, team teaching, and collaboration among faculty who offer separate sections of a multisectioned course. At the intellectual heart of many interdisciplinary programs, we find an interdisciplinary faculty seminar in which a particular interdisciplinary book or issue is discussed at (typically) weekly or biweekly meetings. Such seminars are seldom available to disciplinary faculty whose interdisciplinary involvement is limited to the teaching of general education courses. They promote an intellectual community, expand faculty perspectives, develop interdisciplinary skills, and sometimes even spawn new interdisciplinary courses.

Team teaching may be necessary the first time an interdisciplinary course is taught. In the team's weekly meetings, a variety of essentials get worked out:

the disciplinary perspective underlying each reading; the key points that need to be made and the questions that need to be raised about them in the next week's seminar discussions; and paper topics, exam questions, and "right" answers. The main difference between interdisciplinary teams that prepare faculty for team teaching and interdisciplinary teams that prepare faculty for separately taught sections of the same course is the command required of the perspectives of other disciplines represented in the course. The tendency in courses taught by teams is to let the other person represent her or his discipline. The pressure to develop a sympathetic command of the other perspective(s) is limited to what is required to talk productively with colleagues. When a faculty member is alone in the room with students, he or she needs to be able to present the other perspective(s) sympathetically and convincingly. The consequent demand on team meetings is greater, but the resulting course can be more interdisciplinary than one that is team taught, since faculty model for students how to listen to contrasting perspectives and to think holistically about their integration (Newell, 1983b).

The first task in designing an interdisciplinary course is to identify colleagues in other disciplines that can be called on for collaborative assistance. An interdisciplinary topic takes more than one person's interest, even expertise, because an interdisciplinary course requires multiple perspectives. However broad a faculty member's training may be, it is still a human trait to seek cognitive order, to create a single coherent perspective on how the world works. But contrast if not conflict is essential to interdisciplinary study. To bring two or more perspectives to bear on a single topic, an individual working alone would need to have two minds.

With experience, a single faculty member can design an interdisciplinary course but only after developing sufficient feel for the worldviews, concepts, theories, and methods of relevant disciplines to be able to shift with ease from one perspective to another. Small wonder that interdisciplinarians tend to score high on the tolerance of ambiguity scale of personality tests. It would more fitting to say that they seek out ambiguity. Faculty members who do not have the support of a formal team can still ask colleagues in other departments for assistance. Those who do are often pleasantly surprised, as most faculty are delighted to help familiarize colleagues with their area of expertise. Moreover, those who make such an investment in the interdisciplinary project often become more supportive of the interdisciplinary program as a whole.

Not surprisingly, then, selecting a genuinely interdisciplinary team requires consideration not only of the expertise of possible participants but also of their personalities. For example, one needs to consider whether potential participants are open to diverse ways of thinking, wary of absolutism; able to admit that they do not know; good at listening; unconventional, flexible, willing to take risks, self-reflective, and comfortable with ambiguity. Those who are not may not be appropriate for interdisciplinary teaching (Trow, 1984–1985).

As it turns out, collaboration on an interdisciplinary team is a lot like marriage. One must ask whether the particular mix of personalities proposing a course will work together appropriately. Are the prospective partners discreet as well as knowledgeable? They will learn where the other is most vulnerable or deficient. At least half of the course will deal with material outside one's expertise, which means that one runs the risk of exposing some cherished assumptions as incomplete and misleading if not actually wrong. Values as well as facts become the focus of discussion and debate, so that a partner must be trusted as well as respected. Love is optional.

Participation in an interdisciplinary team can be exhilarating but challenging. It gives the participants an opportunity to see issues from new angles, and, because the underlying assumptions are probed, they can see why others on the team think as they do. One's own perspective is subjected to the same scrutiny, and the holistic spirit of the enterprise requires that one rethink and reexamine it, not merely defend it. Respect for the perspectives of other disciplines is essential. After all, they usually come out of intellectual traditions to which many brilliant people have contributed. Nevertheless, their limitations must be sought out. Faculty members should represent their own disciplines as statespersons, embodying the disciplinary perspective and values but listening as well as contributing to debate, and then, relying on their expanded understanding, voting in the interest of the entire intellectual community.

Try being intellectually playful instead of contentious. Instead of dismissing an uncomfortable idea, hold it up to the light, turn it around, see how it might relate to more familiar ideas. Imaginative play produces unexpected connections, and laughter defuses tension wonderfully. When the perspectives of the disciplines have been set out and examined, let the test of convergent validity set the areas of agreement. Where disagreement remains, avoid dichotomies. They are, as Etzioni (1988, p. 203) puts it, "the curse of intellectual and scholarly discourse." Both-and thinking is the hallmark of the interdisciplinarian and the most promising route to integration.

Selecting a Topic

Successful interdisciplinary courses normally focus on a topic, although the term *topic* should be construed broadly as meaning an issue, theme, problem, region, time period, institution, figure, work, or idea. Within that topic, the most effective strategy is to ask a question that is too broad for any one discipline to answer fully. Since an interdisciplinary course "covers" disciplinary perspectives (typically disciplines or schools of thought) just as a disciplinary course treats subject matter, the course topic needs to be sufficiently narrow to include all relevant disciplinary perspectives. A narrow topic also ensures that these perspectives can be contrasted, because they will all have the same focus. Otherwise, disciplinary contributions will be regarded as merely complementary insights into separate subtopics that can be combined like the pieces of jigsaw puzzle, not as alternative perspectives that need to be reconceptualized before they can be integrated. An interdisciplinary whole is larger than the sum of its parts, and it is complex, not simply complicated. What lends interdisciplinary study much of its challenge and delight is the creative tension that arises from contrasting disciplinary insights. The creative tension is lost if the disciplines are seen as specializing in different parts of the whole, and with the creative tension goes the richness and complexity introduced by the interdisciplinary approach. Many of its interesting educational outcomes are also lost (Fuller, 1993).

The composition of the faculty team severely constrains the range of possible topics. Clearly, there cannot be a serious mismatch between the disciplinary expertise represented on the team and the disciplines claiming to say something important about the topic under consideration. At the same time, one must not conceive of expertise too narrowly. An economist may find it unreasonable to draw on literature or religion if there is no humanist on the team, yet feel familiar enough with the principles of political science (thanks, perhaps, to the rational self-interest model of human nature) that he or she will include that discipline in the course when the team has no political scientist. However, the economist could pay regular visits to a political scientist on campus as the course is being developed to seek advice, tips on background readings, and reactions to the syllabus. In some cases, it may make sense to change the composition of the team, as we did when we added a philosopher with expertise in ethics who had shown considerable interest in the course when approached for advice by a team member. Under ideal conditions, the composition of the team and the course topic would be decided jointly. However, in most cases, one of these factors proves to be more inflexible than the other, which must therefore be adapted to it.

As if this balancing act were not enough, the selection of an appropriate topic must also take student interests into account. Interdisciplinary courses have the potential for motivating students to learn, whether the topic intrinsically interests them or not. When career-minded students are enrolled in required general education courses, that career mindedness can be a major consideration. Successful topics today often deal with issues that are timely and often global (such as ozone depletion), demonstrably relevant to students' careers (such as the American myth of success), or explicitly tied to social problems that affect their personal lives or families—for instance, for students of traditional college age, societal control over their lives; for older married students, teen pregnancy. Even courses that deal largely with other cultures or time periods can be reconceptualized in ways that emphasize their relevance for students' lives. For example, a course on the Weimar Republic could examine the political appeal of Ross Perot. Such courses need to draw on a very limited number of cultures and time periods for the same reasons that limit the number of disciplinary perspectives. Since the appeal of a course may hinge to a considerable extent on the accuracy with which planners evaluate the range of student interests, it may be worthwhile to probe those interests by surveying students or advisers, interviewing a cross section of students, or consulting a student advisory panel.

Differences between the interests of faculty and students become particularly apparent when the topics that faculty propose for interdisciplinary general education courses are highly abstract (for example, The Concept of the Person) or focused on a discipline (for example, Introduction to the Social Sciences). While these topics represent what from the professor's perspective is the "real" course, they have little appeal for students. Such topics as abortion, invasion of privacy by computers, and sexual harassment can lead both to further examine the "real" topics that interest the faculty or meet educational goals and to attracting students' interest.

A substantive topic provides context for abstract issues, glue for the course, and motivation for students. How abstract the topic and how remote it can be from the experience of students depends on an assessment of their intellectual sophistication. For most undergraduates, abstract issues will not capture student imaginations unless the issues are grounded in concrete situations. A way of connecting a course to students' lives is especially important when the students are not particularly intellectually oriented or when they are studying about a different time and place.

Faculty must show students that they need to get behind the commonsense understandings of a topic if they are to explore it adequately. For example, the distinction between the rights of the individual and the rights of the collective can emerge in a class discussion of sexual harassment. Once that distinction (the "real" topic from the perspective of faculty) has been shown to be real and relevant, it can then be examined as a legitimate subtopic in its own right. Readings can be assigned, and students can write papers, but the discussion must always bring insights into the abstract issue to bear on sexual harassment—which in the students' eyes remains the concrete subject.

While academic disciplines are of considerable interest to faculty for a variety of reasons, they are seldom of innate interest to students, for whom they remain vague, abstract labels. If disciplines are not meaningful entities, then neither are courses that take disciplines as their focus. If faculty show students that disciplines contribute valuable insights into topics that do interest them, then those disciplines and their concepts, theories, and methods may start to interest students. When students see that their naive understandings of a topic are inadequate to explain comprehensively what they see, they become more willing to learn something about disciplines that claim to offer explanations of those phenomena.

Identifying Disciplines

One central intellectual task in the process of developing an interdisciplinary course is to determine the appropriate disciplines from which the course needs to draw. Ask of the disciplines selected, Why these and not others? What exactly does the course draw from each? Is there some sense in which disciplines offer different perspectives on the issue? What distinguishes those perspectives? One cannot treat disciplines like beads on a string, where, different as they may be, one is as good as another. Decide on a subtext, that is, on the underlying categories (of assumptions, perhaps) embodied by the disciplines to be included in the course. For example, a course on poverty in America can take as its subtext varying disciplinary assumptions about human nature, such as the priority of individuality, autonomy, or rationality. After determining what each discipline can contribute (and how distinct that contribution is from those of other disciplines), one must decide how many categories the course allows time or space for. A discipline like political science can contribute to a key assumption (say, that people are rational and self-interested), yet it may not be selected for inclusion in the course because another discipline, such as economics, can do an even better job of elucidating that assumption, and there is time for only one discipline.

We must also ask, Is one text as good as another? In an interdisciplinary humanities course on women's expressions of self, do different media allow different facets of self to be expressed? Do they get at the peculiar shortcomings of the definition of women's self in various cultures? Or is the choice merely a matter of a medium in which women are most proficient? A sentence, even a phrase, of explanation about the distinctive contribution that each category of text makes will help to clarify the thinking of faculty and students about the role of these expressive media in the course—and help students to understand why they are studying something like quilts as a form of self-expression. For example, films and music videos could be found upon examination to present essentially similar images of women, whereas none of the literary texts initially selected comes close to their angle of vision.

It is fashionable these days to demand that general education courses pay some attention to ethical issues. However, many of the general education courses taught by faculty who are not philosophers seem content to explore the ethical dimensions of issues in a philosophically uninformed way. Students should become aware of the distinct ethical traditions in our culture: virtue-based, duty-based, rights-based, and utilitarian as well as the emerging, so-called feminist ethic of caring, sharing, and relationships. These traditions often present conflicting demands that complicate our ethical decision making. Students do not need to be exposed to all the variants of these traditions or to get involved in details of the ways in which they are applied, but it does seem important for these courses to make some explicit use of ethical theory. One alternative to the training of all general education faculty in moral philosophy is to use taped lectures by ethicists. Other options include casebooks and guest lectures.

In addition to providing an ethical dimension, the humanities can make distinctive contributions to courses focused on the social sciences. For example, imaginative literature is especially good in providing some empathetic feel for another time or a particular issue, and it can put a human face on a problem, like poverty, that the social sciences tend to hold at arm's length. Biography can reveal how motivations from a variety of sources can come together in a single individual. History can show that the ways things are now are less inevitable than they may seem. For example, a study of the history of attitudes toward abortion reveals that the Catholic church in America did not oppose abortion until well into the nineteenth century. While the humanities seem to emphasize creative expression over patterned behavior, the unique over the predictable, they can play an important role in what would otherwise be exclusively social science courses.

The natural sciences have a role to play in predominantly humanities or social science courses, but that role is often abused. It is easy for the scientists on an interdisciplinary team to think of their disciplines as providing the boundaries or context within which the concerns of the humanities and social sciences are played out—a line of thought that effectively elevates their status within the team. Even nonscientists may agree that science provides facts—the givens with which the other domains of knowledge must come to grips—or that human perceptions and creative expression are subjective, whereas science is objective. However, the history, philosophy, and sociology of science tell us otherwise. Like the social sciences and the humanities, science is a human endeavor that reflects the social and cultural context. In a culture that makes science a secular religion and that enthrones scientists as secular priests, faculty have an obligation to students not to reinforce this myth by presenting science as a fountain of truth and its practice as unproblematic. Instead, insights from the natural sciences ought to be treated like those from other disciplines—that is, as valuable but as limited by their perspective and assumptions. For example, limiting its conception of what is worthy of study and even of what is real to what can be measured directly or indirectly has helped science to develop valuable insights into the portion of reality that it has chosen to study, but that very success has prevented scientists from taking seriously the world of the imaginative, spiritual, or creative.

Developing the Subtext

At the heart of an interdisciplinary course is what I am calling its *subtext*—the abstract issue or issues of which the substantive topic of the course is a particular embodiment. In the preceding example, the subtext underlying a course on poverty is the conflict among the social sciences over the individuality, autonomy, and rationality of human nature or more generally over the possibility of freedom in a deterministic world. For faculty, the subtext is what the course is "really" about. It may be revealed to students at the outset, or it can slowly emerge as the course proceeds, but it is not what motivates their interest—that is the function of the explicit, substantive topic rather than the implicit subtext.

Decisions about selecting a substantive topic, identifying colleagues and disciplines, and choosing texts all need to be informed by the subtext. For a course on poverty in America, faculty need to decide what should be said about the assumptions of autonomy, individuality, self-interest, and rationality that underlie a belief in freedom. Here is where the scholarly challenge to the faculty and the need to consult with experts in other disciplines are greatest, since the relevant professional literatures are seldom organized in terms of such abstractions. Disciplines should be selected that not only have important things to say about poverty but that also embody contrasting assumptions about the autonomy, self-interest, and rationality of individuals. However, the mere contrast of perspectives or underlying assumptions in an interdisciplinary course is not enough. The contributions of diverse disciplines need to add up to something. They need to be integrated into a larger, holistic perspective. Decisions about topic and any subtopics, disciplines, colleagues, and texts have to be decided on both levels—the surface where students are and the subtext level theorized by faculty.

These decisions ultimately have to be made on three levels, because the choice of subtext itself needs to reflect desired educational outcomes. Interdisciplinary courses are really about such matters as recognizing contrasting perspectives; learning how to synthesize, think critically, and reexamine the world that we take for granted; empowering students to tackle meaningful but complex issues; weaning students from dependence on experts without dismissing expertise; and teaching students to value disciplines as powerful sources of insight while becoming aware of the nature of their various limitations. How these concerns fit into the educational goals of the course, not merely the interests of faculty, must guide the choice of subtext.

In general education courses, the choice of educational outcomes is ideally a collective faculty decision, to which faculty responsible for developing courses for a particular requirement must respond. The problem with most general education guidelines is that they are couched in terms so broad as to offer few clues about the specific educational outcomes that are desired. Perhaps in the files of some former chair of a general education committee there are minutes of discussions that clarify just what committee members hoped to accomplish when they ruled, for example, that students must take one course that presents a nondominant perspective. Summaries of the arguments made in meetings where faculty as a whole debated the requirement are even less likely to be available. Thus, even in the general education courses required institutionwide, the choice of educational outcomes is often left up to the faculty members who teach the courses.

This problem is especially apparent with interdisciplinary requirements, because faculty are even less apt to agree on the meaning of *interdisciplinary* than they are on such terms as *global perspective* or *history*. In many cases, a vote for an interdisciplinary requirement appears to have been a vote for innovation, for keeping up with the rest of higher education, or for nontraditional education. Faculty designing interdisciplinary general education courses thus have a special responsibility to think through which educational outcomes are appropriate and to choose subtexts that respond to those goals.

The choice of disciplines must also be informed by the way in which disciplines are used in interdisciplinary courses, since disciplines and not substantive facts are the raw materials of interdisciplinary courses. Almost all first- and second-year interdisciplinary courses provide their own disciplinary base of concepts, theories, and methods instead of stipulating disciplinary courses prerequisites (Newell, 1992). Underlying this base is the perspective or worldview of the discipline. The holistic interdisciplinary perspective develops from the integration of reductionist insights from individual disciplines. This integration is accessible to students only if they can get behind the pronouncements of the discipline on the course topic and understand how those insights have been arrived at. Students need to develop some feel for the worldview of each discipline, and ultimately they need some awareness of the key assumptions on which those worldviews were predicated. Consequently, the selection of a discipline may depend in part upon the feasibility with which the relevant concepts can be derived. If the contribution of physics to the topic is centrally bound up in the notion that mass can be converted into energy, time limitations may preclude even a rough sketch of the basis of Einstein's equation in fundamental physical concepts, and the discipline cannot be included in the course. But simply telling students that $e=mc^2$ does nothing to ground that claim in a scientific worldview. However, if the contribution that physics makes to the topic is focused upon the law of conservation of energy, the discipline of physics can be readily incorporated into that course, since the first law of thermodynamics is already basic and readily grounded in a scientific worldview.

Structuring the Course

The next task is to identify the conceptual glue that holds the course together. The sequence of subtopics or texts that have been selected needs to have a clear-cut rationale that can be communicated to students. In fact, even the best-designed interdisciplinary courses face the problem of making the logic of their structure apparent to students. A thematic thread needs to run through the course connecting individual topics into a coherent pattern. It can provide the context that sets out the disciplinary constraints, or the causal factors, or the background against which the figure stands out. In some cases, the topic itself has some internal logic that can suggest an appropriate sequence of subtopics, but it is more common that the ordering of subtopics will seem largely arbitrary. In these cases, one can turn to the subtext for coherence.

Take the example used earlier of a course titled Perspectives on Women in Western Culture. If the course is to cohere, those perspectives must collectively add up to some theme or subtext. Possible strategies include the contention that there are identifiable historic trends in the ways in which the various arts have portrayed women, that common themes across time and space reflect fundamental distinguishing characteristics of Western culture, or that some art forms are better than others at bringing out particular aspects of the common themes. No matter what argument informs the subtext, the appropriate subtopics, and the texts to be developed, the steps in that argument need to be articulated as precisely as possible, preferably in a written rationale that will also be useful when the course syllabus is drafted and the emerging course structure is reevaluated.

As the course is structured, it is important to keep in mind not only what is being taught but to whom. There are usually a number of reasonable alternatives for structuring an argument, and some arguments will be more educational than others. For example, in a course with a subtext that reexamines key values in American culture, it may be educationally desirable to have the metadiscussions of values grow out of an examination of the values that students see themselves holding (perhaps as the result of a values clarification exercise during the first week), then connecting them to the values of American culture as a whole. This structure would tie otherwise abstract or theoretical discussions to the lives and world of students, motivate them, and bring the lessons home.

In contrast, conceptual coherence in a problem-centered public policy course may come most easily through a course structure that offers a model of how to approach and think a public policy problem through to solution. Following this strategy, the first step is to decide which model to present. One simple model has five elements: It starts with a factual description of the status quo. Next, it makes explicit the values that render it a problem for some people. Then it presents alternative disciplinary analyses of the source of the problem and the recommended solutions flowing from them. Next, it probes the differences in the perspectives (and the underlying assumptions) that lead to such diverse analyses. Finally, it draws on those analyses to restate the problem in a way that is free of the contested assumptions of specific disciplines, develop a holistic analysis, and make an integrated set of recommendations.

The application of this model gets more complex, of course, when the problem is split into subproblems or if the course also undertakes to examine the ideological dimensions and values underlying each perspective. One key decision in structuring a course is the balance between depth and breadth. That is, we have to balance how much of the problem (or how large a problem) we examine against how much we complicate the examination. As the time we spend probing the implicit values or ideologies behind problem definitions or disciplinary perspectives or analyses increases, the time available for exploring the various dimensions or manifestations of the problem itself decreases. Our final decision will probably be based in part on an assessment of the academic strength of the students. Bright or more advanced students can handle depth and complexity. Other students may appreciate broad, substantive coverage.

No matter what the academic strength of the students, it is essential for each analysis to be complicated at least to the extent that students can be shown how the analysis has been arrived at. For example, giving students an assessment of global poverty by a Chicago School economist without explaining the supply and demand curves that underlie his assessment leaves them unprepared for critical evaluation. To choose between competing assessments, they must rely on their own biases, whether these are based on political or social ideology or on religious belief. In such a case, two potential advantages of interdisciplinary education are lost—namely that it helps students to develop the ability to evaluate the testimony of experts through critical thinking and that it thus empowers them to think through complex issues for themselves.

It is tempting to trust that one or a few recurring key concepts can hold a course together. An example from ecology is carrying capacity; an example from cultural materialism in anthropology is human-nature interface; an example from economics is growth with equity. However, such concepts cannot serve as the main source of conceptual glue. After all, concepts typically come out of, and hence reflect, a particular perspective, whether it be that of a discipline or a school of thought. For this reason, concepts alone cannot hold together the different perspectives represented in the course. At best, a concept can signal the coherence of one perspective as it applies to a specific part of the course.

Selecting Readings

It makes sense to start off even the most theoretically sophisticated course with a hook—a reading designed to pique students' interest in the substantive topic, to engage their emotions, and to make the topic real by connecting it with their experiences and their world. For that reason, faculty often start off interdisciplinary courses in the social or natural sciences with something from the humanities—a short story, a play, a poem, or a film. Time is always the chief limiting factor in an interdisciplinary course. Hence, long novels are best avoided.

Especially in the social sciences, it is desirable to assign early in the course a reading that brings home the limitations of students' commonsense understanding of the topic, hence rendering the topic more problematic, and revealing the inadequacy of what up until then had seemed a satisfactory understanding. Students tend to resist social scientific insights as pedantic, jargon laden, or unnecessarily technical until the need for such insights has become evident. Once students have become dissatisfied with their own insights, they tend to be much more open to investing time and effort in learning what the disciplines can offer.

Interdisciplinary courses of any type require readings that reflect the different disciplinary levels. It is clear that every course needs at least one reading on the substantive topic that unmistakably reflects the perspective of each discipline represented in the course. Student motivation and academic background permitting, a reading should be assigned about the role of each discipline—for example, as a particular theory or cluster of concepts—used in the course. The concepts or theory can be explained in lecture (instead of the relatively expensive discussion sections), and their use for this substantive topic can be elaborated and placed in the context of the discipline as a whole. Wherever possible, disciplinary perspectives should be presented by their adherents, whether through readings or lecture. The separate perspectives need to be made explicit in one way or another so that they can be examined by the students. Otherwise, we are asking students to reinvent the wheel, not to learn how to drive vehicles that have already been perfected. Readings must focus on the subtext while directly exploring the more general or abstract issues underlying the course.

How these different kinds of readings are ordered in the course is as much art as it is science. The trick is to anticipate the emerging understanding and interests of students. At what point will they see that they need to learn more about a discipline in order to understand why it advances its arguments? At what point will they recognize (even if the syllabus tells them as much) that the substantive topic is a specific embodiment of a more general issue that now has some interest for them in its own right? At what point will students be ready to pry into the foundation of assumptions upon which each discipline is constructed in order to find out why disciplines arrive at such contradictory conclusions about the same topic? The first time through, one can only guess. The second time provides a much better sense of the problems involved. The standard rule of thumb is that the third time through is the best. After that, faculty tend to get bored, and a new structure if not a new topic is often in order. When in doubt, one can assume that students will be ready for disciplinary insights as soon as their commonsense notions have been challenged and that they will be ready to dig into disciplinary assumptions as soon as two disciplines offer contradictory insights.

Designing Assignments

Evaluative assignments that promote the desired educational outcomes of interdisciplinary study tend to be relational, applied, novel, active, and often connected to self. Students need to learn facts and terms in interdisciplinary courses, and it may on occasion be necessary to use such traditional methods as short-answer questions, definitions, and even—am I saying this?—multiple-choice questions. However, the acquisition of facts is not an end in itself in an interdisciplinary course. Facts, terms, concepts, dates, and so forth are useful as raw material when connections are probed. More appropriate for most purposes, then, are paper topics, essay exams, in-class writing exercises, and discussion worksheets that ask students to decide what facts are relevant to the central task of making some connection, such as that between the insights of two authors, theories, ideologies, value systems, or cultures. At least some assignments ought to ask students to apply course material to their own lives or to put themselves into the course material. For example, in a course on individual freedom in American society whose readings include Plato's *Apology* and *Crito* and Mill's *Essay on Liberty* but nothing on pornography, students could be asked to write an essay on the following topic: "You die of shock from reading this assignment and go to heaven, where you meet John Stuart Mill and Socrates. Engage in a discussion with them on the opposition to pornography in the contemporary women's movement." Students would have to figure out what position each author would take, why and how they would disagree, and where they themselves stood on the issue in the light of those arguments. Volunteers could locate articles on the contemporary debate for distribution in class. Students could even be encouraged to discuss how to answer the assignment among themselves as long as each student writes his or her own essay in his or her own words. While the immediate reaction might be fear, students can have fun with such an assignment, and it would help them to learn about Socrates and Mill, the women's movement, pornography, their own values, and ultimately freedom.

Not all valuable assignments need to be graded. Students can keep reflective journals in which they apply what interests them in the course. These journals can be graded quickly on a pass-fail basis or simply collected and returned. If faculty need a sampling of the journals and make occasional marginal comments, students feel that they are engaging in a dialogue, and little faculty time is invested. To give one illustration, students in a course on success in American society could be asked to keep a journal that chronicles how their views have changed between their first and final essays, both of which address the question, What is my personal view of success, and how do I hope to go about achieving it? The journal assignment could require students to document how each reading contributed to the shift in viewpoint.

Class participation in seminars can usefully be thought of in an interdisciplinary course as an assignment that has some of the burden of moral obligation. Students familiar only with disciplinary courses need to be informed that their role and hence their responsibilities are different in an interdisciplinary course. Because the teacher cannot be an expert, students cannot expect to sit passively at her or his feet. The teacher becomes a guide or coach, the students explorers or active players. Since class discussions become group explorations or team efforts, cooperation is valued over competition. Students hurt only themselves in a traditional disciplinary course when they do not come to class prepared. In an interdisciplinary course, they also hurt their classmates if they cannot contribute their unique insights. When student contributions are seen to be as valuable as faculty contributions, failure to contribute to class discussion becomes immoral—a matter of taking without giving. Consequently, some faculty grade students' class participation. Others find it difficult to make fine distinctions, especially for shy students. In such cases, gross distinctions in class participation can be used as a basis for raising or lowering borderline course grades at the end of a semester.

Two strategies are often used to get discussion started. One is to distribute discussion worksheets on each reading and have students fill them out before class. The other is to spend the first five to ten minutes of class time having students write freely on the topic of discussion for the day. Discussion worksheets afford more reflection. Free writing can help students to shift mental gears from what happened in the preceding period. The relative importance of these two advantages probably varies from semester to semester, depending on students' schedules, and it has to be determined empirically for each class.

In this computer age, it may be possible to require students to run their papers through a spell checker (which picks up most typos as well as spelling errors) before handing them in, which would help to reduce grading time. In order to ensure that students learn from feedback, have them staple their preceding paper to the back of the current one, and inform them that you will read the comments on the earlier paper before you grade the new one. You will tolerate new errors but not the repetition of old errors.

Group papers create a cooperative setting that forces students to confront and then take advantage of the relative strengths of team members. Moreover, students with relatively weak writing skills learn when they work on a computer with four other students while discussing how to structure the paper and word particular passages. Students can be asked to hand in their own individual evaluations of each team member's contribution, including their own. The student culture at any particular institution will determine whether these evaluations should be kept confidential and how they should be used. Unless teammates raise serious questions, the same grade is typically assigned to all team members. This kind of assignment works best in a residential setting. And although commuting students complain bitterly about such assignments, many still participate in them.

It is natural in an interdisciplinary course to ask students to pull the course together in a concluding assignment. However, you should first ask whether they have been adequately prepared for the task. Has class discussion been devoted to integration and synthesis or merely to comparison and contrast? Have students been assigned readings that attempt synthesis, or have readings only offered single perspectives? Have students been shown models of integration or techniques for integration, or have these responsibilities been ducked? General systems, Marxism, and structuralism are only a few of several ready-made models of integration. Pulling it all together is too difficult a task for students to undertake without some assistance. Since it is also the obvious concluding assignment, it behooves faculty to confront the integrative challenge in class.

Preparing the Syllabus

As already noted, making the logic of the structure of an interdisciplinary course apparent to students is a problem even in the best-designed courses. Since there is typically no authoritative textbook (and hence no preface, annotated table of contents, introduction, and opening paragraph within each chapter) to lead students through the course and lay out how each individual section fits with the other, this burden falls primarily on the syllabus (although the message must be reinforced and particularized throughout the semester at the beginning of each lecture or seminar). Nor can the designers of interdisciplinary courses normally rely on a high-school-level course in the subject to orient students to the subject matter of an interdisciplinary course. As a result, course syllabi bear a special burden of explaining what courses are about and why that is of interest.

While some insights should dawn on students gradually as the course progresses, most students find an interdisciplinary course sufficiently confusing that faculty fears of giving away the punch line in the syllabus are simply unfounded. The more explicit the syllabus is about the nature of interdisciplinarity and the goals, objectives, and purposes of the course, the better. The syllabus also needs to spell out the subtext, the logic of the course structure, the disciplines included, and how they are used. Students may not understand these explanations at first, so you should encourage them to reread the syllabus periodically. By the end of the semester, they should have a pretty good idea (albeit in retrospect) of what the course was about.

Spelling out the reasoning underlying the course in some detail also has advantages for faculty. There is nothing like writing something down to clarify your thinking about it and nothing like trying to explain it to a novice to expose the flaws in your reasoning. Try using the syllabus as a developmental tool, drafting and then revising it as the course design takes shape instead of using it merely as a statement of what has been accomplished.

References

Armstrong, F. "Faculty Development Through Interdisciplinarity." *Journal of General Education*, 1980, *32*(1), 52–63.

Davis, A., and Newell, W. "Those Experimental Colleges of the 1960s: Where Are They Now That We Need Them?" *Chronicle of Higher Education*, November 18, 1981, p. 64.

Etzioni, A. *The Moral Dimension: Towards a New Economics.* New York: Free Press, 1988.

Fuller, S. "The Position: Interdisciplinarity as Interpenetration." In S. Foster (ed.), *Philosophy, Rhetoric, and the End of Knowledge: The Coming of Science and Technology Studies.* Madison: University of Wisconsin Press, 1993.

Miller, M., and McCartan, A. "Making the Case for New Interdisciplinary Programs." *Change*, May–June 1990, pp. 28–36.

Newell, W. "The Case for Interdisciplinary Studies: Response to Professor Benson's Five Arguments." *Issues in Integrative Studies*, 1983a, *2*, 1–19.

Newell, W. "The Role of Interdisciplinary Studies in the Liberal Education of the 1980s." *Liberal Education*, 1983b, *69*(3), 245–255.

Newell, W. *Interdisciplinary Undergraduate Programs: A Directory.* Oxford, Ohio: Association for Integrative Studies, 1986.

Newell, W. "Interdisciplinary Studies Are Alive and Well." *AIS Newsletter*, 1988, *10*(1), 1, 6–8. Reprinted in *The National Honors Report*, 1988, *9*(2), 5–6.

Newell, W. "Academic Disciplines and Undergraduate Interdisciplinary Education: Lessons from the School of Interdisciplinary Studies at Miami University, Ohio." *European Journal of Education*, 1992, 27(3), 211–221.

Newell, W., and Davis, A. "Education for Citizenship: The Role of Progressive Education and Interdisciplinary Studies." *Innovative Higher Education*, 1988, *13*(1), 27–37.

Trow, M. "Interdisciplinary Studies as a Counterculture: Problems of Birth, Growth, and Survival." *Issues in Integrative Studies*, 1984–1985, *4*, 1–15.

WILLIAM H. NEWELL is professor of interdisciplinary studies in Miami University's School of Interdisciplinary Studies and director of the FIPSE-funded Institute in Integrative Studies. He serves as executive director of the Association for Integrative Studies, and he is a frequent consultant, evaluator, and lecturer on interdisciplinary general education.

Some principles useful to administrators can be derived from past decades of development in interdisciplinary programs, general education, centers, colleges, and schools.

The Administration and Governance of Interdisciplinary Programs

Beth A. Casey

Two recent developments suggest that we should examine our modes of administering and governing interdisciplinary studies if we are to enhance excellence and productivity. First, interdisciplinarity has achieved mainstream status as recent movements in liberal and general education have emphasized integrative curricula and synthesizing skills and as enrollments in interdisciplinary programs, schools, and colleges have increased dramatically. Second, as the cost of the fragmentation resulting from specialization becomes clear, universities and colleges are seeking to increase coherence and economy through institutional and curricular restructuring.

Administrators seeking to respond to the needs for interdisciplinary instruction and research can benefit by connecting their efforts with plans to increase flexibility for cooperation and collaboration among traditional departments, schools, and colleges and by clarifying their contribution to purposeful institutional mission statements. The procedures and processes involved in administering interdisciplinary programs, which once were considered marginal, will play a new role in higher education in the future.

This chapter presents some principles of program administration deduced from several decades of development in interdisciplinary programs, general education, centers, colleges, and schools. These principles are discussed in terms of institutional contexts and accompanied by suggestions for budgetary supports, faculty concerns, and administrative leadership.

Interdisciplinary Programs

Student enrollment in interdisciplinary programs has increased over the past decade as research has intensified and as needs for development in such areas as women's studies, environmental studies, international and multicultural studies, and science, technology, and human values have been recognized. Newell (1986) tallied 235 interdisciplinary programs. The majority were started after 1971.

In most universities and colleges, these programs continue to "float" on the white space of administrative charts, often reporting only intermittently to the dean of the college. As a consequence, faculty can feel isolated, unsupported, and unrewarded. It is ironic that the administrative units most engaged in integrative study can be isolated institutionally and hence invite cuts when budgets are tight. The development, integration, and support of interdisciplinary programs as models of cooperation and collaboration can be enhanced by observing the eleven principles stated in this chapter.

The first principle is to examine institutional and college mission statements, and make constructive changes emphasizing not only the pursuit of knowledge (the goal of most mission statements) but a cooperative rationality directed toward purposeful—that is, civic or social—ends.

The Human Development and Social Relations Program at Earlham College in Richmond, Indiana, is one excellent example of an interdisciplinary program whose origin and long-term survival owe much to the mission statement of the college. Founded in 1976 to provide interdisciplinary, values-oriented preparation for helping professions as well as a focused liberal education drawing on the social sciences and philosophy, the Earlham program leads to a B.A. degree in Human Development and Social Relations. Nine faculty serve part-time in the program, which offers four team-developed and two team-taught courses: Persons and Systems, and Social Science and Human Values. Four required disciplinary courses form the base on which the interdisciplinary studies (IDS) courses build. Required field study uses experience to further understanding of theories and concepts, and a senior seminar synthesizes theory and practice and bridges to careers. The faculty have primary appointments in specific departments, but the administration supports the program's claims on their time so strongly that no formal joint appointments have been necessary. In line with this first principle—that is, adherence to the institution's goals and mission statement should be part of new interdisciplinary development—program director Nelson Bingham mentioned to me that founders of the program studied the Earlham mission statement carefully in order to integrate themselves with the organization as a whole.

Earlham College was founded in 1847 by the Society of Friends, and Quaker values and ways of doing business permeate its institutional life. The mission statement indicates that the college community must be characterized by mutual caring and respect. Teaching and learning roles merge, and the curricular and the experiential are often combined, so that the college is a sanctuary for reflection as well as a stimulus to practical action. Earlham assumes that "light of truth" can be found in each individual. Hence, policies and practices are developed through consensus building. No single discipline and no single individual is considered able to raise all the appropriate questions, and the curriculum reflects a strong emphasis on interdisciplinary course work and collaborative learning. A service learning program thrives on campus, and 70 percent of the student body spend up to a year in a foreign country studying aspects of the culture and other topics as part of their undergraduate program.

Such a marriage of program and mission statement may be so strong as to be discouraging, particularly for faculty in large institutions. But it is clear evidence of an administrative reality: Those interested in the development of interdisciplinary programs should work toward a mission statement with the kind of ethical praxis that is an inherent characteristic of good interdisciplinary curricula.

The second principle is to establish a council of interdisciplinary programs or some other advisory board to coordinate programs and share problems and ideas. Appoint a coordinator for interdisciplinary programs, possibly an assistant or associate dean, to administer resources, oversee program evaluation, examine annual reports, and evaluate directors on the basis of the recommendations of program advisory committees. Connect this council in some manner (usually it is through a single representative) to the council of chairs in the college and to the general college council if one exists.

The fact that very few such councils exist in universities reflects the generalized institutional fragmentation. A survey in 1983 of interdisciplinary programs at Bowling Green State University uncovered complaints about the absence of joint appointments, unsatisfactory merit evaluations, inadequate resource allocations, and program invisibility. Other state-assisted institutions in Ohio surveyed during the same year revealed similar concerns (Baker and Marsden, 1986), but only one institution was making a systematic effort to provide an administrative structure for program supervision. At Bowling Green, an associate dean for academic affairs now serves as coordinator for interdisciplinary programs, and representatives from the interdisciplinary program council sit on the arts and sciences council and on the council of department chairs. When the interdisciplinary program council was initiated, a fall retreat was held for directors, and several summer institutes were funded for faculty who wished to work on interdisciplinary programs. At present, meetings focus on the sharing of ideas for program planning and advancement.

The best outcome of the interdisciplinary program council has been a new interest in collaboration and funding among programs themselves. For example, the Canadian studies director and the American studies director collaborated on a grant for North American studies, and several directors have joined with two small interdisciplinary departments to form a consortium aimed at developing shared curriculum on graduate and undergraduate levels. Without cooperative interaction, few such endeavors would be forthcoming.

Interdisciplinary General Education

Interdisciplinary curriculum development can fulfill important general education goals. Such curricula help an institution to address common goals and purposes, integrate learning across disciplines, and help students to develop skills essential to life in an interdependent global society, such as the ability to perceive the complex cultural, economic, and political forces that shape our environment. Disciplinary distribution models of general education exist solely to broaden students' education by forcing them to select courses outside their majors. Connection to ethical action and common purposes and understandings is lacking. Moreover, specialized knowledge is increasing so rapidly that students will not be able to accommodate it unless they learn to integrate learning across the disciplines.

The first principle stated in this chapter—a mission statement indicative of a cooperative rationality—is imperative for a general education program that seeks to provide students with the ability to understand different cultures and modes of thought; to investigate the forces that shape the social, scientific, and technological complexities of an interdependent global society; and to assume the social responsibilities that characterize our democratic communities. (Note that the greatest growth in subject matter areas of general education encourages interdisciplinary curricula: international studies; American multicultural studies, including gender studies; and the inherently synoptic curricular areas of historical consciousness and ethical understanding.)

As in the case of interdisciplinary programs, the development and coordination of an integrative general education program requires that a college or universitywide office for general education be established and that it have a director or coordinator. The goal of this office is to ensure that general education development is ongoing, not an activity that takes place only during a periodic ten-year review. A general education committee must have representatives from all colleges and participating departments. It should provide the fulcrum for cooperation and collaboration among competing departments and programs. A program director teaching one-third or one-half time is sufficient in most cases. In small liberal arts colleges, an associate provost or dean might include this among his or her duties. In a very large university, a dean for undergraduate studies might be appointed who, in addition to being responsible for general education, could coordinate advising or administer other parts of the undergraduate curriculum. The formation of faculty development teams or learning communities assembled across disciplines and departments to augment the program and establish a grassroots development is also of the utmost importance. Hence, the third principle of interdisciplinary development is to ground the interdisciplinary general education program in flexible structures for faculty development and plan pedagogical strategies for the implementation of the curriculum. Such a strategy is essential for interdisciplinary development not only because it leads to important changes in student learning but also because it creates a community of learners among the inhabitants of inherently competitive departments (Eble and McKeachie, 1985).

Joseph Tussman (1969), whose interdisciplinary alternative general education program at Berkeley in the 1960s was so influential in interdisciplinary development during the 1970s and 1980s, argued that only in the interdisciplinary faculty community could the awesomeness of the responsibility of liberal education and its essential moral and normative functions be restored. The purpose of his alternate college, he wrote, was "to develop rational powers, to heighten sensitivity to and awareness of fundamental human problems, to cultivate and strengthen the habits and dispositions which make it possible for humanity to displace the varieties of warfare with the institution, the practice, and the spirit of reasoning together" (Tussman, 1969, p. 3).

How does one begin such faculty development enterprises? One example of development under way at Michigan State University, an institution whose size might be thought to preclude such possibilities, is instructive. Michigan State administrators developed an administrative structure to foster integrative development (Greene, 1993). Three centers for integrative studies—in arts and humanities; social, behavioral, and economic science; and general science—are housed in the three core colleges of natural science, social science, and arts and letters. A series of advanced courses at the transcollege level involving all eleven colleges in the university is coordinated by a director of integrative studies, who is aided by a universitywide committee that reports to the provost.

In each center for integrative studies, a director, aided by an advisory committee of faculty and students appointed by each of the core deans, is charged with the responsibility of soliciting new courses from college faculty members. Faculty from two or more departments were encouraged to collaborate in the construction and delivery of courses. The arts and humanities center offers a single multimedia course for all freshmen, America and the World, and a series of fifteen sophomore-level courses, of which one is required. From the courses offered by the center for social, behavioral and economic sciences, students must take one course at the 200 level and one course at the 300 level. All courses offered through the humanities and social science centers and all transcollegiate courses emphasize either national or international cultural diversity. Students also take three courses from the center for integrative studies in general science, and each undergraduate is required to enroll in a three-credit transcollegiate course during the junior year.

Michigan State's system is complex, since it serves a very large university, but faculty development groups or learning communities can be formed in any college or university to support general education development in all curricular areas. Initially, these groups can advise the general education committee on guidelines for skills and understanding in curricular areas. Then the director or coordinator can help the development groups to move to instructional strategies for the curricular area or plans for interdisciplinary course development and curricular coherence. Such groups should allow others to join. Informal luncheon groups can be organized as open forums at which pedagogical strategies can be shared, and faculty with needed expertise can be invited to these meetings. At universities, graduate students who teach course sections are eager to join in the sessions on the development of skills. These groups should also be used as introductions to research on teaching and learning in one's own classroom so that teaching and research can merge in development (Cross and Angelo, 1988).

Learning communities for interdisciplinary development are essential if the goals, structure, and praxis of the curriculum are to be focused as creatively as possible. How will the courses or the program bring the modes of inquiry, techniques, and perspectives of different disciplines to bear upon problems and questions? How are the problems or questions to be defined? How will the gaps between theory and practice be bridged? How will an integrative synthesis be obtained? How and why will the various elements of this synthesis be interrelated? How can collaborative learning groups be introduced into the classroom to resolve these problems through oral and written exercises? How will the processes of reflective judgment essential to interdisciplinary synthesis be taught in the classroom? The complex issues involved in the interdisciplinary enterprise necessitate community building among students and faculty.

Jerry Gaff (1991) has argued that workshops on general education held across the United States and focused on a wide variety of instructional topics—student development models for instruction, computer simulations, writing across the curriculum, multiculturalism, textual analysis, discussion skills, or team teaching—are all relevant to interdisciplinary teaching. In these workshops, faculty intellectual interests are merged with teaching and learning and the development of the academic community. The organization of an interdisciplinary program must receive equal attention. This brings us to our fourth principle: Think as creatively as possible about program logistics, and seek to develop flexible and adaptable structures based on faculty and curricular strengths and student characteristics and needs.

It is not possible to import an innovative interdisciplinary general education program from one institution to the next (Gaff, 1980) because institutional organisms resist implants. The praxis inherent in interdisciplinary development requires each institution to examine its own mission, needs, faculty, and curricular strengths while paying close attention to its historical past. For example, the University of Utah's freshman seminar program is designed to give beginning students depth and continuity in subject matter and opportunities to participate in a close-knit learning community. Senior seminars provide interdisciplinary capstones. While it is unusual for a such a large university to provide an interdisciplinary core of courses, Utah did have a similar development at a much earlier time.

A bank of structural ideas from several institutions can be shared with a developing general education committee in preparation for a brainstorming session for one's own institution in order to assure committee members that other institutions have dealt imaginatively and successfully with interdisciplinary general education. Discussions should focus on general program characteristics rather than on the ways in which they can or should be reproduced in the institution. Hartford University's guidelines for interdisciplinary general education seek to place learning for its students in a contextual frame that unites knowledge and human experience. Thus courses at Hartford focus on living in a social context or on living in a scientific and technological world. In its interdisciplinary courses, Bradford College seeks to link liberal and professional education and the world of work. Harvard's interdisciplinary general education core is scholarly in content, reflecting the preparation of its highly select student body.

Often, a particular religious affiliation in a liberal arts college will suggest fruitful ways of building toward an ethically focused, socially responsible liberal education. Administrators should explore with faculty the characteristics of the student body, the ways in which students best become involved in their academic learning, and the relationship between these concerns and institutional mission and goals. The more the collective values of the institution are taken into consideration, the more carefully and concretely the institution's mission can be focused, and the more possible a satisfactory and supportive program assessment becomes.

An alternative interdisciplinary general education program is often particularly successful in large universities, and it will attract high-quality students. Interdisciplinary general education honors programs typify such an alternative endeavor, and they can be connected to community service, semesters abroad, or internships. The problem of securing faculty to teach in an alternative general education program must be considered carefully before development is launched. Institutional consensus should be sought for all innovative curricular endeavors, and deans and program directors must work to create consensus among department chairs prior to development.

Alternative programs are often formed by coordinating or clustering disciplinary courses and by adding interdisciplinary unifying courses, as in the Federated Learning Community (FLC) at the State University of New York Stonybrook. Students who enroll in the FLC program take three regular courses that offer different disciplinary perspectives identified on the basis of their relevance to a program theme, such as Technology, Values, and Society. The subsequent fourth course is Program Seminar, which provides a small student-centered learning community and seeks to integrate the material for the program courses. Students may use the program as a minor, and the unifying seminar is taught by a faculty member who takes the three other courses as a master learner and then provides participating faculty with feedback on the effectiveness of their courses.

Disciplinary courses can be linked to specially team-taught interdisciplinary courses. Required interdisciplinary capstone programs can offer an interdisciplinary synthesizing experience and can be staffed from within individual departments. It is also possible to design an integrative upper-level core by redesigning existing upper-level interdisciplinary courses to meet general education objectives. The general trend toward interdisciplinary research means that administrators are certain to discover an unusual number of interdisciplinarians closeted in the departments of their institution, and such a resource can become a treasure trove for IDS.

Interdisciplinary Schools and Colleges

At least two kinds of interdisciplinary schools can be formed. The first and most familiar type of institution awards a baccalaureate degree to students who have successfully completed four years of study in a coherent interdisciplinary curriculum that provides an interdisciplinary general education as well as either individualized majors or various interdisciplinary major concentrations. Located within a university or college, such a school most often permits students to combine disciplinary courses with interdisciplinary studies.

The second type of school is a collection of interdisciplinary programs and departments clustered together cooperatively to design and share some interdisciplinary courses and curricula, faculty, and students. These complex structures imply appropriate physical space and often the ability to control the promotion and tenure process for full-time faculty appointments. Such control is important if faculty are to spend time learning other disciplines and developing interdisciplinary research interests.

The fifth and sixth administrative principles emerge from the complexity of interdisciplinary schools and colleges: Seek administrators with experience in interdisciplinary programs to lead such large academic units as schools and colleges, and ascertain that the student's overall curriculum is characterized by coherence and consonance, that is, that there is logical harmony among its parts.

Experienced leadership is essential to stabilize and catalyze an interdisciplinary school or college. The development of interactive structures that encourage the free flow of ideas and the necessity for curricular as well as faculty development are two reasons why experience is needed. Traditional academic departments can inhibit this flow of ideas and create *segmentalism* in industrial organizations. Segmentalism is a condition that keeps any organization from changing and that stifles potential innovation (Kantor, 1983). In particular, administrators need the experience of working through participative teams in order to manage the problems associated with teamwork (Kantor, 1983). Finally, a coherent curriculum must provide breadth, depth, and focus (Zemsky, 1989) as well as some ways of achieving the praxis essential to integrative study in order to assure that the gaps between theory and practice will be bridged.

Miami University of Ohio's School of Interdisciplinary Studies provides an excellent example of a cohesive curriculum and affirms the results of experienced leadership. In 1973, Western College for Women in Ohio faced bankruptcy after 120 years of operation, and its buildings were purchased by

Miami, a state-assisted university of 14,000 students in the town of Oxford. A planning committee at Miami formulated several proposals for use of the newly acquired campus, one of which was a residential interdisciplinary college. A School of Interdisciplinary Studies offering a Bachelor of Philosophy of Interdisciplinary Studies and setting its own degree requirements was approved (Newell, 1984). Over the past twenty years, the school has attracted excellent students.

In the freshman and sophomore years, students participate in a residential learning program and take a required core of three interdisciplinary courses: one in Creativity and Culture, one in Natural Systems, and one in Social Systems. The freshman year focuses on the concepts and methods of the natural sciences, social sciences, and humanities and arts through integrative themes that connect the disciplines and compare and contrast world views. A fourth course links the three required courses and provides experiential learning. In the sophomore year, since all students have some grounding in the disciplines, faculty offer relatively ambitious interdisciplinary courses (Newell, 1984). The Natural Systems faculty teams may examine world food and health problems, and the Creativity and Cultures teams may offer courses on the spirit of the age or on comparative cultures.

Students take one or two courses from other university divisions each semester of the freshmen and sophomore years, and in the middle of the sophomore year they plan individualized majors. Junior seminars—one offered in each domain—concentrate on the methods of interdisciplinary research and specific interdisciplinary approaches that will strengthen the background that students need in order to complete individualized majors.

In 1993, in a development that may occur in other colleges and universities as restructuring to promote economic cooperation becomes essential and as trends toward interdisciplinary research and teaching flourish, several interdisciplinary departments and programs at Bowling Green State University (BGSU)—the American Studies, Film Studies, and Women's Studies programs and the department of Ethnic Studies—agreed to join together to form a School of Cultural Studies coordinated by a committee with a revolving chair. All four units have few undergraduate majors and very large enrollments in general education courses.

New research in Cultural Studies linking the humanities and social sciences makes it productive for their faculty to design courses together and to share scarce new tenure track positions through dual appointments. There are no plans at the moment for these programs and departments to form a single unit under a director, and each unit remains independent and offers a degree in Cultural Studies in its own area.

Of the interdisciplinary colleges formed in the 1960s and 1970s, The Evergreen State College (TESC) in Olympia, Washington, has perhaps the best record of continued success in maintaining and developing its original goals for collaborative interdisciplinary learning. A public college founded in 1971,

TESC presently enrolls about 3,200 students. In its mission statement of 1990, TESC directs that all teaching and learning experiences shall be characterized by interdisciplinary learning communities that immerse students in a diversity of perspectives and foster development of the skills of cooperation, communication, and integration. Required internships and applied projects bridge theory and practice, and independent study options and self-evaluations reinforce the requirement that students take responsibility for their own learning.

The TESC Coordinated Studies programs, which have faculty teams of two to five members and forty to a hundred students, focus on particular themes or topics, such as Political Economy or Human Development. Advanced-level curricula were formed around the specialty areas that were discovered to be essential and attractive to the student population, such as Environmental Studies; Science, Technology, and Health; or Political Economy and Social Change.

A closer look at TESC's success suggests our seventh principle of good practice: Develop nonhierarchical administrative structures, and increase commitment and ownership by decentralizing decision making.

Critical debate and evaluation of the outcomes of interdisciplinary teaching must take place if a school, college, or program is to respond adequately to student needs. Nonhierarchical structures encourage criticism and honesty in assessment. As the hierarchy of authority increases, the rate of innovation decreases (Seymour, 1988).

Departments at TESC were avoided to assure that faculty would join together to create coordinated studies, and the first central committee on governance was termed the Disappearing Task Force, a name still used for primary policy-recommending committees that are dissolved after they complete their tasks. The most radical of the measures adopted at TESC to reduce hierarchy was the rejection of a system of tenure and ranking. A system of differential faculty contracts is under review, while a set salary scale based exclusively on years of experience remains the system of monetary reward. According to comments to me by Barbara Leigh Smith, academic dean, the system just described has had no adverse effect on the institution's ability to attract excellent faculty. Deans and the provost base their determinations about retention on evaluations by students and faculty members with whom faculty members have worked. The goal of collegiality typifies such a system.

Interdisciplinary Centers and Institutes

Disciplinary implosion, specialization, and the rapid growth of interdisciplinary research and teaching have caused centers and institutes to proliferate on college and university campuses. It is not unusual for the largest universities to have a hundred such units. Centers and institutes have a number of benefits. They foster collaboration among departments and programs; enable collaborators to recruit and retain important faculty; increase and strengthen research and funding possibilities; serve community, state, and national governments; create new areas of specialization; and foster institutional prestige and program visibility (Ikenberry and Friedman, 1972).

If administrators are to allocate sufficient resources for these units and develop sound policies for the evaluation and compensation of faculty participation, they need to ensure that such centers and institutes have been fully integrated into the life of the university or college as a whole. The development of policies and sound organizational criteria for performance and the selection of leaders for units become central administrative tasks. A central advisory board should coordinate the centers and institutes and oversee periodic reviews aimed at evaluating the way in which the missions of individual units have been integrated into the mission of the university. The faculty who serve on this board should include individuals who hold seats on other significant decision-making bodies, such as the faculty senate or graduate council.

This suggestion gives rise to the eighth principle of good practice: Seek directors for centers and institutes who can integrate their units into the mission of the institution, manage interdisciplinary teams, create visibility, and establish purposeful identity for their programs.

Those who direct such centers today are often entrepreneurs with strong funding capacities, who can create conflict both within the institute or center and within the university or college that it serves. An academic administration can counter their influence by appointing leaders with the capabilities just listed.

In a quest for criteria for assessing interdisciplinary centers or other administrative organizations, Ernest Lynton proposes that (1) administration assure that the organizational and budgetary procedures facilitate and enhance genuine cooperation and interaction among faculty in carrying out research and instructional activities, and (2) the process of resource allocation as well as the criteria for evaluating and rewarding faculty performance reflect the importance of the interdisciplinary activity. Lynton notes as well that internal as well as external relationships must provide ongoing and close contact with state-of-the-art research in each component discipline in order to ensure up-to-date interdisciplinary work of the highest quality (1985, pp. 146–147).

This leads us to the ninth principle of good practice: Think creatively about the ways in which interdisciplinary centers and institutes can be used to foster the collaboration and community interaction that are often absent from faculty research and teaching.

Both disciplinary implosion and the need to service relationships between the university and the community were factors that gave birth to new interdisciplinary programs. Centers of medical ethics or of social philosophy and policy emerged from philosophy departments. Political science departments created centers for public administration or public policy. Science, engineering, or technology departments and programs have given rise to centers for environmental study, materials science, and biotechnology. Most faculty today experience structural barriers to academic excellence in both research and teaching, and they benefit greatly from centers and institutes that foster interaction and collaboration.

For example, the Commission on the Humanities (1990) at the University of Chicago recommends the creation of opportunities for faculty to restructure their traditional disciplinary tools and frameworks of questioning. Chicago once addressed this issue by organizing committees to support graduate students and faculty members who were doing interdisciplinary research and who could not be accommodated in departments. However, these committees often lacked flexibility, and they were difficult to dissolve once they had been formed. To improve interdisciplinary research, the commission at Chicago took four steps. First, it proposed the formation of consortia among departments. For example, the departments of English and Romance languages could decide to create a European literature steering committee to coordinate appointments between departments and sponsor lectures and conferences of common interest. Second, it proposed the creation of groups inspired by successful interdepartmental workshops focused on graduate research—temporary structures whose purpose was to bring faculty and graduate students together. Any gathering of faculty could designate itself to the dean as such a group and subsequently sponsor workshops or design programs. Groups were to have a life of three to five years, after which time they were required to ask for renewal. Third, it proposed the creation of centers to bring in visitors, support leaves for faculty within the university, and hold research seminars. Fourth, it proposed the organization of a humanities institute to serve as a home for the consortia, groups, and centers and as a meeting ground and source of services for humanistic scholars at the university. Chicago was successful in creating a new flexibility, and centers and institutes were built from the creative ferment that the groups and consortia had fostered.

Faculty Concerns and Budgetary Support

The deployment of faculty in interdisciplinary programs, centers, institutes, general education programs, or schools poses an organizational challenge to administrative leaders that requires innovation and careful attention to policy development. Budgetary resources for programs must be discovered and defended, and procedures to assess and supply needs must be developed. If interdisciplinary units are coordinated and aligned in ways that enhance cooperation and enrollments and if they are integrated into the structure and mission of the organization as a whole, administrators will find it much easier to defend and support them.

The most difficult problem for interdisciplinary programs and the coordinators and directors of centers and general education is that they have to borrow faculty from departments. Only schools and colleges that have their own control over tenure and promotion escape this difficulty. This is why interdisciplinary programs have to fear for their lives when financial times are tough, and such fear is rational if the institution lacks sound program coordination and assessment and a well-focused mission that includes interdisciplinary study and research. Directors must beg faculty from department chairs, whose responses often seem arbitrary. The flow of faculty into and out of programs is foreign to departments whose membership is traditionally fixed, and it requires support for time-flexible appointments and evaluations for tenure, promotion, or merit salary. Hence, the tenth principle of good practice is to create policies that enable both probationary and tenured faculty to hold joint and term appointments. At the least, concrete understandings about time sharing and about receiving fair and equitable evaluations must be established.

Regular joint appointments can be made when a faculty member will render substantial service both to a department and to an interdisciplinary program or center on a permanent basis. Renewable joint appointments can be made when a faculty member will render service for a specified period of time. More informally, it may be possible for a dean, a chair, and a program director to agree that a percentage of instructional time will be written into the annual contract of a faculty member who wishes to participate in an interdisciplinary program while being assigned to a tenure track within the department without the formality of a term appointment. Such a flexible appointment is sometimes made when an interdisciplinary program is new or when it does not yet show the stability deemed necessary for term or dual appointments.

In regard to reappointment for a probationary faculty member, the program coordinator, with assistance from tenured faculty on the executive advisory council, could prepare a written assessment of the probationer's strengths and weaknesses in the areas of teaching, research, and service. The department of actual appointment applies the reappointment policy that it has in place and adds the program assessment to the accumulated record that is presented to the tenured faculty who vote on the reappointment. The chair prepares a letter for the probationer summarizing the strengths and weaknesses identified by faculty in both groups, specifies the vote of the tenured faculty in the department, and shares the letter and this information with the dean and the executive advisory committee in the interdisciplinary program. Both chair and program coordinator can then discuss the reappointment recommendation with the probationer before it is forwarded to the chief executive officer.

The last principle helps with the difficult problem of funding interdisciplinary centers, programs, or institutes fairly: Develop a plan to assess the instructional outcomes and, where relevant, the research productivity of interdisciplinary units.

When directors and deans seek support, they need to present a clear and comprehensible assessment of their unit's research and instructional productivity to administrators.

To augment budgetary support, administrators may find it possible to establish a special fund for faculty willing to participate in instruction and research in interdisciplinary units. Participating faculty are, of course, pursuing their own instructional and research interests, but they are also going beyond the learning of their home disciplines. Interdisciplinary work emerges from state-of-the-art research in component disciplines. It may be possible to set aside a small amount of money to be used for academic purposes, such as travel to conferences, special bookstore purchases, and reprints. The award of a stipend of any size, however slight, implies commitment to interdisciplinary programs and recognition of intellectual exploration beyond the recipient's base discipline.

Leadership

Deans, directors, and coordinators of interdisciplinary schools or programs are confronted with a stimulating challenge. All administrators must have interpersonal skills, but interdisciplinary leaders also need the ability to form and work through participative teams. They must stimulate followers to become leaders, develop faculty ownership, and manage the problems associated with teamwork. Leadership as partnership is part of the interdisciplinary task, and it is assumed that leaders themselves will be competent interdisciplinary teachers and scholars. However, more than other types of administrators, they may also need to understand the cultural differences among faculty members associated with different fields.

For example, the research of Gaff and Wilson (1971) on cultural differences among faculty associated with different fields noted that faculty from education and the fine arts encouraged group participation, while faculty from engineering and mathematics were less inclined to do so. The investigators concluded that the focus and structure of faculty's pedagogical style increased as a function of the degree to which knowledge in the field was codified.

Many universities and colleges today have a bureaucratic culture that assumes consensus and discounts controversy because it threatens organizational stability. Interdisciplinary leadership taps motivational bases and creates a climate in which risks can be taken and uncertainty and ambiguity are considered to be essential to the work that takes place. By seeking praxis and emphasizing experiential learning and the world of work, interdisciplinary leaders break open some of the customary boundaries of the university or college and establish what one writer has termed the *virtual institution*—that is, an institution that "marshals more resources than it currently has on its own, using collaborations inside and outside its boundaries" (Godbey, 1993, p. 38). Such leadership will increasingly be in demand as colleges and universities find it necessary to cooperate and share resources both within and without.

References

Baker, K., and Marsden, M. "Structuring for Success: A Progress Report on Administering the Political, Economic, and Pedagogical Realities of Interdisciplinary Programs." Paper presented at the National Conference on Interdisciplinary Baccalaureate Education, Columbia, South Carolina, 1986.

Commission on the Humanities. *Report of the Commission on the Humanities at the University of Chicago.* Chicago: University of Chicago, 1990.

Cross, P., and Angelo, T. *Classroom Assessment Techniques.* Ann Arbor: University of Michigan Press, 1988.

Eble, K. E., and McKeachie, W. J. *Improving Undergraduate Education Thorough Faculty Development: Analysis of Effective Programs and Practices.* San Francisco: Jossey-Bass, 1985.

Gaff, J. "Avoiding the Potholes: Strategies for Reforming General Education." *Educational Record,* 1980, *50,* 50–59.

Gaff, J. G. *New Life for the College Curriculum: Assessing Achievements and Furthering Progress in the Reform of General Education.* San Francisco: Jossey-Bass, 1991.

Gaff, J., and Wilson, R. "Faculty Cultures and Interdisciplinary Studies." *Journal of Higher Education,* 1971, *3,* 186–201.

Greene, J. T. "Integrative Studies Core Program at Michigan State." *Association for Integrative Studies Newsletter,* 1993, *15,* 1–4.

Godbey, G. "Beyond TQM: Competition and Cooperation Create the Agile Institution." *Educational Record,* 1993, *74,* 35–42.

Ikenberry, S. O., and Friedman, R. C. *Beyond Academic Departments.* San Francisco: Jossey-Bass, 1972.

Kantor, R. M. *The Change Masters: Innovation and Entrepreneurship in the American Corporation.* New York: Simon and Schuster, 1983.

Lynton, E. "Interdisciplinarity: Rationales and Criteria of Assessment." In L. Levin and I. Lind, (eds.), *Interdisciplinarity Revisited: Reassessing the Concept in the Light of Institutional Experience.* Linkoping: OECD/CERI, 1985.

Newell, W. "Interdisciplinary Curriculum Development in the 1970s: The Paracollege at St. Olaf and the Western College." In R. M. Jones and B. L. Smith (eds.). *Against the Current: Reform and Experimentation in Higher Education.* Cambridge, Mass.: Sehenkman, 1984.

Newell, W. *Interdisciplinary Undergraduate Programs: A Directory.* Oxford, Ohio: Association for Integrative Studies, 1986.

Seymour, D. *Developing Academic Programs.* Washington, D.C.: AAHE-ERIC Higher Education Report, 1988.

Tussman, J. *Experiment at Berkeley.* San Francisco: Jossey-Bass, 1969.

Zemsky, R. *Structure and Coherence: Measuring the Undergraduate Curriculum.* Washington, D.C.: Association of American Colleges, 1989.

BETH A. CASEY is coordinator for general education and special programs at Bowling Green State University. She is a former assistant dean at Hobart College and William Smith College, where she assisted in the development of an interdisciplinary general education program. She teaches American and English Canadian literature and publishes on general education, academic administration, and the humanities; she is often a consultant on the development of interdisciplinary curriculum.

Assessment procedures vary widely from local to national models.
This chapter surveys and evaluates recent developments in the
assessment of interdisciplinary studies.

Assessing Interdisciplinary Learning

Michael Field, Russell Lee, Mary Lee Field

The outcomes assessment movement of the last decade has had a major impact on American higher education. There is no shortage of good books and essays, both theoretical and practical, on the topic. Many of these works are described in the bibliography that concludes this chapter. But, while much of the information in these sources will be useful or even essential to those who must develop and implement systematic assessment of an interdisciplinary program, nowhere will these individuals find a concise discussion of assessment tailored to interdisciplinary studies.

Providing such a discussion is our task. We begin with a brief review of contexts and problems. Next, we document the ways in which some programs have used a variety of assessment techniques to measure and document the outcomes of interdisciplinary study. We do not propose these examples as textbook models or ideal programs. Rather, by showing how assessment acts in practice, they illustrate both the wide range of appropriate activities and some of the difficulties involved in doing assessment well. Since we focus on the how of assessment, we do not provide data or summarize assessment results for the programs that we describe. In line with the emphasis of this sourcebook on practice, we end the discussion with a list of suggestions: four dos and three don'ts for the assessment of interdisciplinary programs. The chapter concludes with an annotated bibliography.

Contexts and Problems

The conduct of a well-conceived assessment for interdisciplinary programs poses some unique problems. One cornerstone of systematic assessment is the measurement of progress toward clearly and operationally defined goals. To a

New Directions for Teaching and Learning no. 58, Summer 1994 © Jossey-Bass Publishers considerable extent, the nature of the goals and their underpinning learning concepts determines the methodology that will be selected. Student mastery of the knowledge base and key concepts of a discipline may be easy to assess from the technical standpoint if there is considerable agreement across institutions and across the nation about the knowledge base and the key concepts. For example, take an undergraduate program in psychology. One major goal of many such programs is to help students to be accepted by and succeed in graduate school. Since graduate programs have largely agreed on required elements in their curricula and since the Graduate Record Exam in psychology has traditionally established measurement areas, an undergraduate program can measure the success of its students relative to students trained in other undergraduate psychology programs by using nationally normed instruments.

The conceptual format for such assessment is knowledge of established curricular areas. Nationally normed tests are available for most established areas of the curriculum. For example, the Educational Testing Service (ETS) offers nationally normed major field achievement tests in fifteen disciplines. As a result, established disciplines have difficulty finding assessment techniques for learning goals only when goals are unique to a particular program or to a small number of programs. Interdisciplinary programs tend by their very nature to be unique. No standard curriculum provides an index against which students' acquisition of knowledge can be measured. Moreover, many of those who teach in interdisciplinary programs would find the acquisition of knowledge a questionable measurement goal. Not surprisingly, then, a recent task force found few standardized tests that were appropriate, given the numerous differences that exist between interdisciplinary programs (Doty and Klein, 1990).

No common intellectual base unites interdisciplinary programs, which range from honors and women's studies programs to entire liberal education curricula. In an informal, unpublished research project, the Association for Integrative Studies (AIS) examined the range of claims made for interdisciplinary courses and programs and concluded that what links interdisciplinary approaches is not typically content but rather process. The AIS found that interdisciplinary approaches are often designed to produce some or all the following outcomes in students: tolerance of ambiguity or paradox; sensitivity to the ethical dimensions of issues; the ability to synthesize or integrate; enlarged perspectives or horizons; creativity, original insights, or unconventional thinking; critical thinking; a balance between subjective and objective thinking; humility; sensitivity to bias; an ability to demythologize experts; and empowerment. However, such outcomes are rarely described explicitly.

While the lack of a standard curriculum in interdisciplinary programs is usually thought of as a major disadvantage for the assessment of interdisciplinary education, it may be a major advantage in that it requires us to focus on the development of intellectual capability in the student rather than on a fixed body of information (Lawrence, 1991). Intellectual maturation and cognitive development may in fact be the most appropriate conceptual frameworks for assessment in interdisciplinary education. A view of academic progress based on "talent development" (Astin, 1991, p. 6) would draw on the work of established developmental theorists. Although some standardized instruments have been constructed to reflect developmental themes (for example, Rest, 1986), the unique characteristics of most interdisciplinary programs suggest that assessment methodologies tailored to a particular program may be preferable to standardized instruments. In fact, the few documented examples of successful assessment of interdisciplinary programs tend both to exemplify a developmental perspective and to prefer locally designed measures over standardized or nationally normed instruments.

The Western Program

One of the most widely respected interdisciplinary programs in the nation, the School of Interdisciplinary Studies at Miami University of Ohio, which is sometimes referred to as the Western Program, provides an interdisciplinary, residential undergraduate program that serves in part as an alternative to the general education distribution requirements that most students must fulfill. Although the Western Program began its assessment efforts with several nationally normed standardized tests, its staff have moved increasingly to qualitative measures, such as portfolio analysis, in which faculty review the collected products of student effort for evidence of student development and for congruence between programmatic goals and perceived outcomes (Hutchings, Marchese, and Wright, 1991).

The Western Program has developed a complex series of procedures to measure the impact of interdisciplinary education on its students. First, faculty are asked how well prepared their students are. The fact that interdisciplinary courses are widely accepted at Miami University, often in place of disciplinary core requirements, is an indirect measure of their effectiveness. Second, students are pre- and posttested with the COMP instrument, which is described later in this chapter. Third, the nationally normed College Student Experiences Questionnaire is administered to measure students' self-reports of their academic behavior, including how often they discuss ideas out of class, revise papers, read books, change their opinions, and so on. Fourth, data that are already available, such as percentile rankings of seniors on Graduate Record Examinations and the Law School Admissions Test, are consulted. Fifth, graduates are asked to evaluate their education. Since a standard, nationally normed alumni assessment instrument published by the American College Testing Program is used for this purpose, program managers can compare the reactions of graduates with those of other graduates across the country. Sixth, students are asked to assemble comprehensive portfolios of their work, and program managers conduct yearly student interviews so that they can merge their sense of what students are learning with students' own sense of the experience (Newell, 1992).

The Evergreen State College

The Evergreen State College (TESC) has undertaken an ambitious research project to explore student learning in a highly interdisciplinary institution stressing a coherent learning community that offers a powerful combination of social and academic experiences. The methodology for these assessment efforts is based on a developmental theory described by William Perry (1970). He argues that students typically move through epistemological and ethical stages of increasing sophistication. Attempting to measure student development in terms of progress through these stages, TESC researchers used an essay instrument called the Measure of Intellectual Development to perform both cross-sectional and longitudinal studies of student growth between the freshman and senior year. Like the Western Program at Miami University, TESC also makes extensive use of student portfolios and locally designed measures (Thompson, 1990).

The original TESC methodology (Thompson, 1990) made use of data that were already available when the assessment program began, namely data on cognitive development in freshman programs compiled by the Washington Center for Improving Undergraduate Education and data from student self-evaluations that the registrar's office had been collecting for some time. The use of existing data serves as a model for others who wish to set up an assessment program. Data collection can be quite time-consuming and require a high degree of cooperation from others, some of whom may be resistant to the very idea of assessment. If data already exist and their use is appropriate, they can produce some interesting and valuable results. The use of such data certainly does not preclude the setting up later of a sophisticated longitudinal study. TESC's approach, which is ambitious in scope and imaginative in nature, combines qualitative and quantitative measures. The school's efforts at quantitative measurement in particular illustrate the immense difficulty of conducting a sophisticated assessment of intellectual development in an interdisciplinary program.

One rather unusual set of data available to TESC researchers consisted of scores on the Measure of Intellectual Development (MID) pretest (version A) and posttest (version AP) obtained principally from freshman students in four TESC core programs in the 1986–87 academic year. The MID consists of a series of essays scored to classify student responses according to Perry's (1970) scheme. These data allowed investigators to compare the progress in cognitive development of TESC students in their freshman year with that of students at other institutions for which MID norms in the freshman year were available. The fact that the pre- and posttests were not paired created a methodological problem. TESC investigators later used student self-evaluations to estimate developmental levels for seniors in order to approximate cognitive development over a four-year period.

The registrar's office at TESC has collected thousands of faculty and student evaluations, which are used instead of grades, and essays called "The Student's Own Evaluation of Personal Achievement." These data were tapped for what Thompson (1990) calls a "retrospective longitudinal study" in which the essays were read and rated by the same method as the MID. Scores derived from the portfolio material were then compared with scores from seniors at other institutions who had completed the MID.

Significantly, TESC studies did not attempt to analyze research material for specific academic skill measures, such as the development of vocabulary or of logic, or for knowledge in traditional academic majors. Although one goal of the curriculum may well be the development of specific knowledge, what sets an interdisciplinary program apart from other programs is often an emphasis on integration: Cognitive growth can be a strong indirect measure of the ability to integrate. Although TESC research is vulnerable to criticism on methodological grounds—Thompson (1990, p. 6) himself says it is in the "Rube Goldberg tradition of applied social science"—the results have nevertheless been useful enough that the staff continue an ongoing effort to document the intellectual development of TESC students.

In 1992, TESC published a report of a second large retrospective study of its students, again using their narrative self evaluations (Thompson, 1992). Researchers chose to study the whole population of 165 students who had entered as freshmen and then graduated between 1986 and 1988. While it is possible that these "indigenous" students do not represent all TESC students, since transfer students were excluded, the researchers wanted to be able to measure changes over time as the result of the TESC curriculum. Thus, they needed to follow students from their first year through their senior year. This time, the research focused both on writing and on cognitive development. The research involved analyzing the writing samples according to three scales: composition—a measure of syntax, grammar, organization, and style; communication—a measure of what the Educational Testing Service (1990) refers to as *rhetorical effectiveness*; and cognitive complexity, which again called for scoring as in the Measure of Intellectual Development (Thompson, 1992). With this model of assessment, the researchers were able to look at writing in the context of cognitive development rather than as an isolated factor.

Wayne State University

Like the programs at Miami University and TESC, the interdisciplinary studies program (ISP) at Wayne State University has maintained a developmental focus and relied primarily on locally developed instruments for its assessment strategies. The ISP serves a student population of 55 percent female, 50 percent African-American working adults who have an average age of forty. ISP faculty began the assessment process by researching what constitutes viable assessment in interdisciplinary programs. Then they set about designing an assessment plan that would respond both to the traditional views of assessment often expressed by institutions and to the concern voiced by faculty that inappropriate, standardized instruments would be imposed. The resulting ISP document states that assessment is formative, interactive, student and program centered, and based on a conceptual framework that respects students, curriculum, and faculty. The resulting plan, still in the first stages of implementation, illustrates how a nontraditional program housed in a traditional university setting can build on research, adhere to its own goals, and address the tensions raised by assessment issues.

A major feature of the ISP assessment plan is its comprehensive nature. It includes entry-level, ongoing, and exit-level assessment processes.

Entry-level assessment makes use of holistic and standardized assessment instruments, including the ACT ASSET, the Nelson-Denny reading comprehension instrument, RPS (a reading progress scale), and an experimental learning goals inventory. The Interdisciplinary Studies Seminar, a required entry-level course, addresses the educational goals of the students and the program and explains the nature of interdisciplinary study. Most entry-level assessments are administered during this course.

For ongoing assessment, a number of courses are using student portfolios. This effort is still in its early stages. A systematic approach to portfolio analysis is under development. A long-established, rigorous, writing-intensive requirement serves as a capstone experience for students, either in a senior essay/project course or a senior seminar. Students' oral presentations of their writing to a faculty panel provide an important opportunity for exit-level assessment.

In the process of identifying and instituting appropriate assessment of student learning, the ISP has established three more goals for the development of a full assessment plan. First, assessment must supply data on graduates. Specific types of data are important for ongoing program and student outcomes assessment. The school's first goal is to develop a data base of its more than 2,000 graduates. Data on students' application for, acceptance into, and completion of graduate programs will be added to this data base. Current, informal data indicate that more than 50 percent of the ISP's graduates go on to graduate school in a variety of programs. The systematic collection of data on their performance in those programs will provide increasingly reliable information.

Second, the instruments used must be locally designed. Programs need to adapt current methods to fit their own needs. At the same time, they need to recognize how program, student, teacher, and institutional goals are sometimes conflated. The ISP is developing exit interview and self-assessment instruments for graduating students. Given the maturity and experience of the ISP student body, these interviews and assessments will provide a wealth of data for analysis. The caution here, both for the ISP and for other programs that adapt or create such instruments, is to be clear about the goals that are to be assessed. Students' goals may not exactly match those of the institution or even the program.

Third, assessment must yield regularly updated data that are readily accessible. The ISP is beginning to regularize, store, examine, and analyze the data that entry-level standardized tests, university-administered math and English tests, and writing samples in the computer conferencing activities have already collected. Plans call for those data to serve as a baseline reference for exit-level assessment.

An overarching goal of program assessment, one tenaciously attended to by the ISP, is that assessment must be interactive with faculty and program goals, especially in regard to curriculum development. In response to data generated by ISP assessment efforts and to issues raised in discussion about assessment, existing courses have been revised, new courses have been proposed, and a revised set of graduation requirements has been drafted.

Despite such positive results within the program, the process has not always gone smoothly. Ideas about quantitative assessment are embedded in decades of tradition and practice. Indeed, one could say that the assessment movement has been driven by such assumptions. ISP faculty, who are wary of standardized tests, which they believe are biased toward younger students straight out of high school, and unconvinced that quantification can provide a valid measure of complex intellectual development, continue to discuss, experiment with, and labor to refine an assessment plan that responds to and adapts current research to their own curriculum and students.

Types of Instruments

While assessment at the Western Program, TESC, and the ISP at Wayne State University combines quantitative and qualitative measures, these institutions all display a marked preference for locally designed, qualitative approaches. Qualitative measures have some real advantages. That faculty are involved in their design means that faculty recognize their value and appropriateness for local assumptions and needs. Moreover, you do not have to pay a testing company to administer or interpret an instrument that a local committee has designed. Faculty and students are often suspicious of the quantification, elaborate statistical explanations, and surrender of autonomy that usually accompany standardized instruments.

However, while locally designed assessment instruments are often attractive to faculty and have special benefits for highly distinctive interdisciplinary programs, standardized instruments also have some real advantages. If a standardized, nationally normed instrument is available and if it is a valid measure of some of the educational goals of an interdisciplinary program, results may be more convincing to skeptics than the results of a locally designed instrument. The increased credibility stems in part from the sophisticated statistical treatment that the testing company generally provides. Moreover, standardized tests make meaningful comparison with other programs possible.

A noteworthy example of a standardized test that is sometimes useful to interdisciplinary programs is the College Outcomes Measures Project (COMP) developed by the American College Testing Program as a measure of student learning in general education. While general education programs are usually disciplinary, the COMP instrument is nevertheless useful in an interdisciplinary context because it is designed to measure a wide range of intellectual skills rather than specific intellectual content.

To design the instrument, the American College Testing Program asked a large number of colleges and universities to submit general education outcomes statements, and to these it added outcomes statements found in the published literature. A system of factor analysis was used to narrow the broad range of general education concerns to six major areas that the COMP instrument would test: Functioning Within Social Institutions, Using Science and Technology, Using the Arts, Communicating, Solving Problems, and Clarifying Values.

Those who wish to add a standardized assessment instrument to their assessment package have several other tests to choose from, at least in the United States. The General Intellectual Skills test, still in development by the Educational Testing Service, will measure critical thinking and communication skills. The instrument will use grading by local faculty members equipped with detailed protocols designed by the ETS. A somewhat more disciplinary ETS instrument, the Academic Profile, measures college-level reading, writing, mathematics, and critical thinking in relationship to the humanities, social sciences, and natural sciences. Both long and short forms are available. Reports from the ETS can compare results with those from a normative group of similar institutions.

Several other measures of critical thinking have appeared in recent years, although many are not standardized and lack sufficient supporting validity and reliability research (Alexander and Stark, 1986). For example, the Test of Critical Thinking attempts to test five dimensions: defining a problem, selecting information relevant to the problem, recognizing stated and unstated assumptions, formulating and selecting relevant hypotheses, and drawing valid conclusions. While Lehmann (1963) found critical thinking scores to increase between the freshman and senior years, which suggests that the Test of Critical Thinking does measure changes related either to college persistence or to maturation, there has not been much validation research. Another critical thinking instrument, the Reflective Judgment Interview, is designed to measure the development of complex reasoning and judgment skills, using a Perry-like (Perry, 1970) scheme of intellectual development. The Reflective Judgment Interview also suffers from a lack of validation research. A third critical thinking instrument, the Watson-Glaser Critical Thinking Appraisal Test, is intended to measure three dimensions: inference, deduction, and recognition.

While standardized, quantitative instruments can be useful, they do have serious limitations. A great deal of what is important in the life of a university and in particular of interdisciplinary programs is difficult or impossible to measure quantitatively, and it certainly cannot be measured by a single test. It is tempting to attend rather to what can be easily measured than to what is at the heart of our academic enterprise. If the assessment movement is to prove useful rather than destructive to interdisciplinary programs, educational values must determine the shape and nature of our assessment efforts, not the reverse.

Suggestions

The suggestions that follow result from our examination of the efforts of institutions to assess their interdisciplinary programs. For simplicity's sake, we have formulated these suggestions as dos and don'ts. We propose the following four dos:

First, when designing and implementing an assessment program, pay special attention to the culture of the institution and to the political dynamics that help to determine whether new efforts succeed or fail.

Second, articulate the goals for assessment of the program early in the development process, and compare them with the goals of assessment professed by the larger institution. Differences in philosophies and perspectives can lead to difficult confrontations later on, especially if they have not been made explicit.

Third, be sure to incorporate feedback loops into your assessment program so that assessment can lead back to improvements in teaching. Data collection and interpretation are useless if no changes result from what has been learned.

Fourth, use multiple measures. Every kind of assessment method has both problems and benefits. Try to incorporate a mix of appropriate instruments and methodologies into your program, for example, by complementing locally designed measures with some standardized measures.

Our experience suggests three don'ts for the developers of assessment programs:

First, do not start assessment with a major, complex program that requires more expertise and resources than are available. Begin with a few potentially useful assessment activities, and see how well they work.

Second, do not confine assessment responsibilities to a sector of the university isolated from most other faculty and students. Even if your campus has an institutional research office to coordinate assessment efforts, faculty should still be involved in assessment, especially at the policy level.

Third, do not tie assessment to faculty evaluation in any way. Faculty are almost certain to resist any such linkage, and it has few or no compensating benefits.

Interdisciplinary Program Assessment: An Annotated Bibliography

The materials described in this section are of two kinds: on the one hand, major articles and research on the assessment element of interdisciplinary programs; on the other, a variety of other documents that should aid faculty and program officers. Given the dearth of materials dealing specifically with assessment in interdisciplinary programs, the resources listed here, even if they do not specifically mention interdisciplinary studies programs, will prove useful by providing models, perspectives, guidelines, information, ideas, cautions, and encouragement as faculties tackle assessment mandates.

Academic Profile II. (brochure) Princeton, N.J.: Educational Testing Service, 1988.
   Describes the ETS assessment service for general education.

Alexander, J. M., and Stark, J. S. *Focusing on Student Academic Outcomes: A Working Paper.* Ann Arbor, Mich.: NCRIPTAL, 1986.
   A detailed summary and analysis of existing assessment instruments.

American College Testing Program. *COMP Technical Report 1982–1991: Clarifying and Assessing General Outcomes of College.* Iowa City: ACTP, 1992.
   Reports on research relevant to the COMP instrument.

Angelo, T. A., and Cross, K. P. "Faculty Goals and Roles: Bringing Assessment into the Classroom." *CAPHE Connections,* Fall 1989, pp. 5–6.
   Reports the results of a survey of thirteen colleges with the Teaching Goals Inventory (see Cross and Angelo, 1990). Makes inferences about the linking of teaching goals to assessment.

Association of American Colleges and Universities. *A New Vitality in General Education: Report of the Task Force on General Education.* Washington, D.C.: AACU, 1988.
   Focuses on the reasons for and scope of general education.

Association of American Colleges and Universities. *Program Review and Educational Quality in the Major: A Faculty Handbook.* Washington, D.C.: AACU, 1992.
   A comprehensive, practical guide, with a bibliography, to the process of setting up a program review. Lists the key elements of strong programs, gives

questions to ask when setting up a review, and addresses specific assessment issues. Does not deal specifically with interdisciplinary studies programs, but still highly useful.

Assessment and Accountability in Higher Education. Proceedings of Conference, December 5–7, 1989. Denver, Colo.: Education Commission of the States, 1990.
Summarizes themes and findings from the conference. Includes the program of presentations and recommendations.

Assessment in Learning Communities. Olympia, Wash.: Evergreen State College and Washington Center for Improving the Quality of Undergraduate Education, n.d.
Describes programs in learning communities that operate under the aegis of the Washington Center for Improving the Quality of Undergraduate Education. Assesses student values instruments, reviews programs, and reports on use of the Measure of Intellectual Development. Has an interdisciplinary focus.

Astin, A. W. *Assessment for Excellence: The Philosophy and Practice of Assessment and Evaluation in Higher Education.* New York: American Council on Education and MacMillan, 1991.
Reviews assessment methods, philosophies, and public policy implications. Little discussion of interdisciplinary programs, but essential reading on the assessment movement.

Belenky, M., Clinchy, B., Goldberger, N., and Tarule, J. *Women's Ways of Knowing: The Development of Self, Voice, and Mind.* New York: Basic Books, 1986.
Advances a developmental theory of women's intellectual maturation.

Cross, K. P., and Angelo, T. A. *Teaching Goals Inventory.* Berkeley: School of Education, University of California, 1990.
Provides a fifty-two-question instrument for identifying teachers' goals.

Doty, W. G., and Klein, K. T. (eds.). "Interdisciplinary Resources." *Issues in Integrative Studies,* 1990, 8 (special issue).
A collection of articles by leaders in the field that includes the "SVHE Task Force Report on IDS," which has a section on assessment.

Edgerton, R. "Assessment at Half Time." *Change,* September–October 1990, pp. 4–5.
Defines some political issues inherent in mandated assessment.

Educational Testing Service. *Rhetorical Effectiveness Scoring Guide for Reflective Essay.* Emeryville, Calif.: ETS, 1990.

Presents a rating scale originally devised to rate high school seniors' reflective essays.

Erwin, T. D. *Assessing Student Learning and Development: A Guide to the Principles, Goals, and Methods of Determining College Outcomes.* San Francisco: Jossey-Bass, 1991.
Chapter One has a section on the emergence and purposes of outcome assessment. A good overview, but interdisciplinary courses are not discussed.

Ewell, P. *Assessment and the "New Accountability": A Challenge for Higher Education's Leadership.* Denver: Education Commission of the States, 1990.
Details current issues and political complexities of assessment.

Ewell, P. "Assessment and Public Accountability: Back to the Future." *Change,* Nov.–Dec. 1991, pp. 12–21.
An overview of trends and problems that pays special attention to federal assessment initiatives. Argues that pressures for change are still strong.

Field, M., and Lee, R. "Assessment of Interdisciplinary Programs." *European Journal of Education,* 1992, 27(3), 277–283.
Discusses assessment in interdisciplinary programs. Defines obstacles, discusses standard instruments, and makes recommendations.

Forrest, A. *Time Will Tell: Portfolio-Assisted Assessment of General Education.* Washington, D.C.: American Association of Higher Education, 1990.
Analyzes the problems and strengths of portfolio-assisted assessment, lists resources, and provides guidelines.

Gaff, J. G. *New Life for the College Curriculum: Assessing Achievements and Furthering Progress in the Reform of General Education.* San Francisco: Jossey-Bass, 1991.
Examines reforms in general education. Chapter Three provides some information on outcomes assessment in a variety of programs.

Hutchings, P., and Marchese, T. "Watching Assessment: Questions, Stories, Prospects." *Change,* September–October 1990, pp. 13–38.
Describes the assessment programs at several universities and analyzes assessment trends of the preceding four years. Does not focus directly on assessment of interdisciplinary programs.

Hutchings, P., Marchese, T., and Wright, B. *Using Assessment to Strengthen General Education.* Washington, D.C.: AAHE Assessment Forum, 1991.
Provides useful information on the assessment of general education programs, but no mention of interdisciplinary studies.

Lawrence, B. M. "Assessment of Student Development in Interdisciplinary Programs and Courses." Paper presented at the Association for Integrative Studies Conference, Minneapolis, 1991.

Sets up a three-tier plan for the development of assessment programs: Define the purposes of assessment, define goals for program and students, and choose the conceptual framework.

Lehmann, I. "Changes in Critical Thinking, Attitudes, and Values from Freshman to Senior Years." *Journal of Educational Psychology*, 1963, *54*, 305–315.

Analyzes a battery of cognitive and affective tests, including the Test of Critical Thinking, administered to 1,051 freshmen and seniors to determine whether receptivity to new ideas increases with progress through college.

Manley, J., and Jacobs, R. *IGE Programs Assessment: California State Polytechnic University*. Pomona: California State Polytechnic University, n.d.

Articles about the Cal Poly program, including "Enhancing Quality by Assessment: A General Education Project." Also provides a good model for a program assessment document.

Marchese, T. J. "An Update on Assessment." *AAHE Bulletin*, Dec. 1987.

Chronicles the assessment movement and provides an overview of its problems and needs. Makes a strong argument for diversity and rich, integral forms of assessment.

McGlenney, K. M. "Whither Assessment? Commitments Needed for Meaningful Change." *Change*, September–October 1990, p. 54.

Defines four key issues in assessment.

MEAP Secondary Classroom Assessment Task Force. *Classroom Assessment*. Lansing: Michigan Department of Education, 1990.

Three memos addressed to Michigan social studies teachers, language arts teachers, and science teachers. Each memo contain packets of classroom assessment tools and information about assessment techniques. Useful information about secondary school practice in Michigan.

Musil, C. McT. (ed.). *The Courage to Question: Women's Studies and Student Learning*. Washington, D.C.: Association of American Colleges and Universities, 1992.

Investigates how and what students learn in women's studies classes by using different forms of assessment at different locations. Describes a range of approaches and methods for assessment.

Musil, C. McT. (ed.). *Executive Summary of* The Courage to Question. Washington, D.C.: Association of American Colleges and Universities, 1992.

Condenses the original 213-page report into twelve pages. May be useful as an introduction to the full report.

Musil, C. McT. (ed.). *Students at the Center*. Washington, D.C.: Association of American Colleges and Universities, and National Women's Studies Association, 1992.
A collection of essays by the members of a FIPSE-sponsored team engaged in a three-year project focused on the assessment of women's studies. A valuable discussion of assessment in nontraditional settings.

Newell, W. H. "Academic Disciplines and Undergraduate Interdisciplinary Education: Lessons from the School of Interdisciplinary Studies at Miami University, Ohio." *European Journal of Education*, 1992, 27(3), 211–221.
Discusses interdisciplinary teaching at Miami University's School of Interdisciplinary Studies. The discussion includes some description of assessment efforts.

Outcomes Assessment in Higher Education. (brochure) Princeton, N.J.: College Boards and Educational Testing Service, 1989.
Describes the instruments developed by the College Boards and the Educational Testing Service.

Paulson, C. "State Initiatives in Assessment and Outcome Measurement: Tools for Teaching and Learning in the 1990s." In *ECS Working Papers*. Denver: Education Commission of the States, 1990.
Uses information gathered from a ten-page questionnaire to describe state assessment plans. Michigan's description is quite general and vague.

Perry, W. *Forms of Intellectual and Ethical Development in the College Years*. New York: Holt, Rinehart & Winston, 1970.
Presents a complex, multistage scheme for understanding cognitive development among male college students.

Rest, J. *Moral Development: Advances in Research and Theory*. New York: Praeger, 1986.
Discusses the nature of moral development and how it can be measured.

Sims, S. *Student Outcomes Assessment: A Historical Review and Guide to Program Development*. New York: Greenwood Press, 1992.
Discusses student outcomes assessment from historical and design perspectives.

Thompson, K. *Learning at Evergreen: A Study of Cognitive Development Using the Perry Model*. Report No. 1. Olympia, Wash.: Evergreen State College Assessment Study Group, 1990.
Details Evergreen's early efforts in outcomes assessment.

Thompson, K. *Learning at Evergreen II: Writing and Thinking.* Report No. 2. Olympia, Wash.: Evergreen State College Assessment Study Group, 1992.
Uses student portfolios to analyze changes in the written expression and cognitive development of Evergreen students.

University of Maryland University College Plan for Assessment of Undergraduate Learning Outcomes. College Park: University of Maryland, 1989.
Describes the assessment program at University College, an interdisciplinary program with some similarities to the ISP at Wayne State University. Available from David Montgomery, vice president for academic affairs.

Using Portfolios at Indiana University: A Report from the Portfolio Subcommittee of the Intercampus Committee on the Assessment of Writing, Barbara Cambridge, Chairperson. Unpublished paper. Indianapolis: IU/PUI, 1989.
Explains the rationale, history, implementation, development, and application of the program at Indiana University. Includes a good set of questions about setting up such a plan.

Valeri-Gold, M., Rolson, J. R., and Deming, M. P. "Portfolios: Collaborative Authentic Assessment Opportunities for College Development Learners." *Journal of Reading,* 1991, 35(4), 298–305.
Explains how portfolios can be used in formative assessment of students' progress.

Wepner, S. B. "On the Cutting Edge with Computerized Assessment." *Journal of Reading,* 1991, 35(1), 62–65.
A description of computerized assessment packages. While these products have been designed specifically for the assessment of reading at the K–12 level, they provide good detailed information useful in a college setting.

Werner, P. H. "Assessment: Review of *Integrated Assessment System* by R. Farr and B. Farr." *Journal of Reading,* 1992, 35(5), 416–418.
Reviews an extensive and flexible system for the assessment of language arts developed by the Psychological Corporation. Summarizes that system, which applies primarily to K–12 instruction but is applicable at the college level.

White, E. M. "The Damage of Innovations Set Adrift." *AAHE Bulletin,* November 1990, pp. 3–5.
Details failures in ambitious programs and provides thoughtful warnings. Interdisciplinary study is not singled out for comment.

MICHAEL FIELD is professor of English and director of the honors program at Bemidji State University. He served as head of an AIS task force on the assessment of interdisciplinary learning.

RUSSELL LEE is professor of psychology at Bemidji State University. With Michael Field, he coauthored an invited article on the assessment of interdisciplinary learning for the European Journal of Education.

MARY LEE FIELD is associate professor of humanities in the interdisciplinary studies program at Wayne State University. She has headed assessment projects in that program, and she adds a cross-cultural perspective resulting from her teaching posts in Greece, Japan, China, and the former Yugoslavia.

*This chapter analyzes the need and possibilities for interdiscipli-
nary networking. It identifies issues that can hamper such networking, and describes hands-on strategies that can build effective
interdisciplinary networks.*

Organizational Networking: Taking the Next Step

Nelson E. Bingham

A group of lions and a group of tigers were confined to an area in which food
was lacking. The tigers, solitary animals that they are, spread out to isolated
territories. In contrast, the lions remained together in a single pride and hunted
cooperatively for food throughout the entire area. Eventually, hunger drove the
lions to attack the only source of food left—the tigers. As each tiger was over-
powered, killed, and eaten, the remaining tigers scattered throughout the available territory. Eventually, there were no more tigers.

The contemporary context for interdisciplinary studies is perhaps not
quite as threatening. Still, the moral of the story—cooperation or networking
enhances one's ability to resist external threats—can be applied to interdisciplinary programs and organizations struggling for survival in the largely disciplinary world of higher education. The future of interdisciplinary studies
depends in no small part on our ability to create effective networks among the
increasing number and variety of interdisciplinary programs and organizations
that have arisen in recent years. The preceding chapters have presented some
important strategies for strengthening interdisciplinary endeavors. To the
extent that those strategies succeed, individual interdisciplinary programs and
single interdisciplinary organizations will benefit from the power offered by
improved networking.

In this chapter, the term *networking* refers to interconnections between
interdisciplinary organizations. To some extent, such interconnections now
occur when individuals are members of multiples. For example, members of
the Association for Integrative Studies also belong to the Association of General and Liberal Studies, the National Collegiate Honors Council, and numerous other groups. However, there is almost no integration at the organizational

level. Most members of an interdisciplinary organization, such as the American Society for Environmental History, know little or nothing about other groups, such as the Society for Human Ecology, that share the same concerns. Yet integration is the most distinctive feature of those engaged in interdisciplinary work. Interdisciplinary organizations, then, need to begin acting more like lions than like tigers. We must begin to use our propensity for integration not just in our academic endeavors but also in our political and interpersonal efforts.

The population of organizations that identify themselves as interdisciplinary is large, diverse, and growing. Each group has a distinct aim and mission and serves a reasonably well-defined constituency. Nevertheless, all groups have certain qualities in common. One is the commitment to an integrative mode of thinking, which is manifest in the tendency to make connections across the usual disciplinary boundaries, to see values and actions as tightly linked, and to tie abstract theory and practical experience together. Perhaps as an outgrowth of their synthetic thinking, interdisciplinarians are also likely to use metaphorical language to describe their activities, particularly metaphors of organisms and living systems. The present chapter exemplifies that tendency.

Another shared element is the experience of operating outside such traditional structures as administrative units in higher education and ways of organizing materials in the library. This outsider status constitutes a common field of resistance that forms the ground on which diverse groups have had to function. Thus, the academic body has resisted each new interdisciplinary organism as if it were an invading virus. New ways of approaching inquiry, theory, and application of knowledge have been perceived and responded to as a threat to the integrity of the prevailing disciplinary structure. This shared context represents an important reality for all interdisciplinary organizations.

Conceptual Definition of Networking

How can we facilitate the integration needed? First, we must develop a richer array of networks. Networking is a complex, ongoing process. There are also many forms of networking. Individuals who have memberships and other kinds of involvement in multiple interdisciplinary organizations provide one level of linkage. Such connections now exist, but no one knows how extensive they are. A survey of the membership of the Association for Integrative Studies (AIS) identified fifty-eight other interdisciplinary organizations to which at least one member of the AIS belonged. These other organizations included the American Studies Association; the National Association for Science, Technology, and Society; and the Society for Values in Higher Education.

The process of organizational networking can begin as an individualistic enterprise, with each separate organization agreeing to cooperate as a means of furthering its own agenda or mission. However, a broader identity could emerge in the long run. Such an identity could emphasize the larger framework of interdisciplinary studies as a distinct approach to knowledge and its application. The Association for Integrative Studies embodies this framework, since its identity is not defined by topical content or by a focus on any specific area of application.

What exactly is this distinct approach? Interdisciplinarity necessarily involves a sense of interconnectedness. This sense manifests itself in three stages. These three stages roughly parallel the three major levels at which the field of psychology operates—knowledge (or cognition), attitudes (or affect), and action (or behavior).

First, we gain increased knowledge of other groups. The process begins with increased communication, which heightens our awareness of other entities (cultures, disciplines, interdisciplinary organizations) and deepens our understanding of our similarities with and differences from them. For example, the Society for Human Ecology has been very willing to exchange its publications with other groups that indicate parallel interests.

Second, we build positive feelings of respect for other groups. As the sharing of information proceeds, we become better able to identify common interests. This commonality can be perceived in terms of theory or methodology or even of shared sociological or political contexts. For example, it might make sense for the American Society for Environmental History and the North American Association for Environmental Education to cooperate in pursuit of their shared goals.

Third, we share activities and resources with other groups. These resources typically include membership and mailing lists. Fruitful sharing of such information could occur, for example, between the Friends Association for Higher Education (a Quaker organization) and the International Christian Studies Association. Increased cooperation in joint activities is closely related. One common vehicle is the joint conference, such as the one held by the Friends Association for Higher Education and the Friends Council on Education at Guilford College in 1988.

Some Core Issues in Networking

Some basic building blocks for networking may already exist. Even so, those who attempt to construct even modest networks of apparently similar organizations, let alone a meganetwork of all those interested in interdisciplinary studies, will confront a number of key issues.

One issue is clustering. How can interdisciplinary organizations be grouped so as to highlight common interests? One approach is to cluster them under five general heads: organizations that deal with higher education in general (example: the Society for Values in Higher Education), organizations that focus on a specific area of curricular concern (example: the National Collegiate Honors Council), organizations that emphasize linkages between traditional disciplines (example: the Society for Literature and Science), organizations that study a specific group of people (example: the National Women's Studies Association), and organizations that have a specific topical focus (example: the Society for Human Ecology).

Another issue is inclusion or exclusion. Should networking include everyone? If not, who should be excluded? Should all levels of educator be included, or should our networking involve only those in higher education? Should interdisciplinary networks include practitioners, or should networking involve only theoreticians?

In the case of interdisciplinary networking, the decision about inclusion or exclusion will be particularly salient as it relates to the definition of interdisciplinarity. This thorny question for all interdisciplinarians is brought immediately to the foreground by the networking process. Some will argue for maximal inclusiveness—incorporate anyone into the network who, knowing its membership, wishes to participate. However, other interdisciplinarians will argue with equal fervor that the interdisciplinary paradigm requires some boundaries if it is to achieve academic legitimacy. One highly successful organization based on exclusivity is the American Association for the Advancement of Science, which has a careful process for according affiliate status to other organizations.

Some effective mini-networks can arise in the various regions of this inclusion-exclusion continuum. One good example is the International Federation for Systems Research, an organization of groups concerned with systems research. Such smaller-scale networks should be nurtured, since any effort at large-scale networking across the disciplines will require considerable progress in addressing this particular issue.

The other issue that is likely to emerge is territoriality. The norm in academe today is a struggle for existence, and even disciplines and disciplinary organizations must fight to survive. Interdisciplinary organizations face the same reality. Indeed, the survival instinct may be an important countervailing force to the tendency of interdisciplinary organizations toward integration. This survival instinct can be manifested as territoriality, which can take the form of a reluctance to share membership lists or to cooperate with other, seemingly similar organizations.

As the story of the lions and tigers shows, an overdeveloped sense of territoriality can be maladaptive. Such feelings can probably be dealt with only through the patient building of personal connections that will allow trust to grow between key players in the different organizations. At present, personal connections are developing among such organizations as the National Collegiate Honors Council, the Association for General and Liberal Studies, the Association for Integrative Studies, the Society for Values in Higher Education, and the American Association for Higher Education.

Networking Strategies

The very definition of networking implies some possible strategies for networking. At the most basic level—developing a sense of interconnectedness—relationships should be built among those involved in pertinent interdisciplinary organizations.

Initial Contacts. The first contacts can occur spontaneously as representatives or leaders of various organizations meet through consulting visits, at conferences, or by working together on some common enterprise. For example, a member of the board of the Society for Human Ecology could participate in the National Women's Study of Social Problems. An interdisciplinarian who wishes to promote networking should always take advantage of opportunities to discuss common interests with members of other interdisciplinary organizations.

Personal Follow-up. The next step is personal follow-up, which can occur through correspondence or E-mail, although it must also include face-to-face contacts through mutual visits and attendance at the conferences of the other organization. For example, the annual conference of one group could organize a panel of representatives from several kindred organizations. Such an event would give the leaders of participating organizations added opportunities for both formal and informal interaction. As an alternative, two or more organizations could arrange for a meeting between their governing boards, executive directors, or other leaders.

Organizational Interaction. Once some level of relationship exists among the leaders of two or more organizations, other steps will be appropriate. These can include an exchange of organizational information (newsletters, journals, and so forth) or the sharing of membership mailing lists so that information can be shared with members directly. Reciprocal representatives can be appointed to serve as liaisons at the conferences of other organizations.

Expansion of Personal Interchange. As members of different organizations become more aware of their counterparts in other groups, natural networks will begin to emerge. Such a phenomenon is often seen on computer bulletin boards.

Formal Ties Between Organizations. More formal steps could also be taken. Two organizations might offer dual memberships at a somewhat reduced rate—an effective means of counteracting the tendency toward territoriality. Or, if two organizations regularly have annual conferences at different sites around the country, they might coordinate their planning so that the two meetings would not take place in the same region in a given year. Such a step would not only minimize the competition between the organizations but give interested members an opportunity to attend at least one of the conferences if they could not afford the expense of travel to both. As an alternative, the organizations could sponsor a joint conference at the same site.

Organizational Collaboration. Ultimately, two or more organizations could cooperate on various projects—publishing a joint journal issue, seeking a grant for some endeavor, or lobbying together for some political issue.

Networking with Undergraduate and General Education Organizations

Many organizations serve the needs of undergraduate and general education. The leading organizations include the Association for General and Liberal Studies, the National Collegiate Honors Council, the National Association for Core Curriculum, the Society for Values in Higher Education, the Association of American Colleges and Universities, the Meiklejohn Education Foundation, the National Society for Internships and Experiential Education, and the Association for Integrative Studies. Since these groups share a common interdisciplinary approach—a common concern for pedagogy, student learning, assessment, and values—and since they also face common patterns of resistance, it is evident that they need to network among themselves.

A collaborative effort could attract far more attention to these concerns than the isolated work of any one group. However, such action can take place only after the attitudinal or feeling level of relationships and the knowledge or cognitive level of information sharing have developed considerably.

Networking with Specialized Organizations

A review of any listing of interdisciplinary organizations reveals that most such groups tend to focus on a particular topical area—a subset of people (women, ethnic groups), a specific area of application (technology, child development), or a content area (the environment, religion, systems research). For most of these specialized areas, there are already several organizations. For example, at least five groups are interested in "technology": the Society for Philosophy and Technology; the Society for the History of Technology; the Society for Social Studies of Science; the National Association for Science, Technology, and Society; and the Humanities and Technology Association. Since many members of these organizations belong to several such organizations, there is much potential for cooperation at the organizational level.

Here is one illustration of effective networking: The American Institute of Biological Sciences (AIBS), an umbrella federation of forty-five scientific societies and research laboratories, publishes journals and newsletters, sponsors joint conferences, and speaks in a unified voice for its member organizations in the public arena. The AIBS works both to enhance education and research in biological science and to strengthen working relationships among various biology professional societies. One of its major goals (which all member organizations seem to share) is a commitment to understanding and preserving biodiversity. While the AIBS is not really an interdisciplinary network, it does show what such a network might look like.

One of the most exciting aspects of the possibilities inherent in such a model is the annual joint conference at which a dozen or more separate organizations meet at a common site and sponsor some common sessions as well as their own distinct programs. The 1991 conference of the AIBS included such groups as the American Fern Society, the Botanical Society of America, the Ecological Society of America, and the Organization for Tropical Studies. These organizations collaborated in organizing conference workshops and presentations on the topic of science education.

Conclusion

One can imagine a future in which a number of vital networks crisscross interdisciplinary studies. These networks facilitate communication and effective cooperation among all those committed to an interdisciplinary approach, whether their emphasis is on teaching, research, or application. Such a future is within our grasp, but it will require serious attention to the tasks identified in this sourcebook. Moreover, the pursuit of those tasks will benefit from the strengthening of networks.

As Klein notes in Chapter One, interdisciplinarians must work to identify and acquaint themselves with a rapidly growing body of interdisciplinary knowledge. To do so, they must go beyond the usual bibliographic search techniques to locate sources outside traditional publication channels and traditional categories of knowledge. The organizational networking described in this chapter promotes such broad search processes, and a wider appreciation of interdisciplinary knowledge will suggest new directions for networking.

Integration is at the heart of the interdisciplinary enterprise. It is exciting to envision the possibilities that can emerge as the integrative process extends from the classroom to the administration of programs, to the interdisciplinary body of literature, and ultimately to the professional organizations that provide the sustaining framework for interdisciplinary teaching, research, and application.

NELSON E. BINGHAM is professor of psychology and NEH Chair in Multidisciplinary Studies at Earlham College, where he has taught since 1974. Former director of Earlham's interdisciplinary program in human development and social relations and past president of the Association for Integrative Studies, he has done extensive research on psychological development in Japan, and he has consulted with various colleges on interdisciplinary programs.

INDEX

ORDERING INFORMATION

NEW DIRECTIONS FOR TEACHING AND LEARNING is a series of paperback books that presents ideas and techniques for improving college teaching, based both on the practical expertise of seasoned instructors and on the latest research findings of educational and psychological researchers. Books in the series are published quarterly in spring, summer, fall, and winter and are available for purchase by subscription as well as by single copy.

SUBSCRIPTIONS for 1994 cost $47.00 for individuals (a savings of 25 percent over single-copy prices) and $62.00 for institutions, agencies, and libraries. Please do not send institutional checks for personal subscriptions. Standing orders are accepted.

SINGLE COPIES cost $15.95 when payment accompanies order. (California, New Jersey, New York, and Washington, D.C., residents please include appropriate sales tax.) Billed orders will be charged postage and handling.

DISCOUNTS FOR QUANTITY ORDERS are available. Please write to the address below for information.

ALL ORDERS must include either the name of an individual or an official purchase order number. Please submit your order as follows:
    Subscriptions: specify series and year subscription is to begin
    Single copies: include individual title code (such as TL54)

MAIL ALL ORDERS TO:
    Jossey-Bass Publishers
    350 Sansome Street
    San Francisco, CA 94104-1342

FOR SUBSCRIPTION SALES OUTSIDE OF THE UNITED STATES, CONTACT:
    any international subscription agency or Jossey-Bass directly.